The Rise of the Abundance Economy
A Spiritual Journey as told by Dr. Gary L. Sorensen

Painting by Gary Sorensen Age 26

© COPYRIGHT 2021 Gary L. Sorensen
All Rights Reserved.

Contents

Preface

Chapter 1   1
Personal Experiences, Observations and Revelations 1958-2021

Chapter 2   23
The Favor Path

Chapter 3   31
Covenant Relationships

Chapter 4   35
Alignment of Assignments

Chapter 5   39
Agreement and Collaboration

Chapter 6   43
Awakening Consciousness

Chapter 7   57
Abundance Economic Models

Chapter 8   67
Abundance Companies and Organizations

Chapter 9   149
Conclusion

Preface

I thought it all began one day when I stopped at an out-of-town gas and convenience store and was blankly staring through the glass door at the selection of bottled water choices. At first I was amazed at the variety of brand choices, quickly followed by the variety of pricing offered. The duration of my stare allowed my subconscious to ponder and formulate a question to propose to my conscious mind that was momentarily stuck in neutral. The proposition was "When did we begin paying for water?"

Little did I know at the time that this simple question would become a "burr in my saddle" that would eventually lead me into a deep and revelatory journey into the realm of economics. That "burr" gradually expanded the initial question into "When did we begin to pay for food, for clothing, for housing, for transportation, for fuel, …for anything." In fact, I was not even aware of the journey until I saw the approaching signpost that announced "now entering The Rise of the Abundance Economy."

The journey has been more a process of both looking back over a lifetime and looking forward and observing rather than an exercise in deep thinking. It has been much more a personal travelogue of thought, inspiration and revelation than any attempt to organize or promote a textbook of economic theories. The journey is my story as told from the perspective of my life experience from age 8 to 72. It has only been as I have noticed all the beads of pearl on my lifetime necklace that I appreciate the journey.

The journey is told from my perspective and vantage point. It is not religious but it is spiritual because I am a spiritual being living in a secular world. The intent is to provide a road map to lead someone from where they **are** to where **IT is**, with landmarks that may act as points of reference or points of interest. The **IT** being a revelation of a **REALM of Reality** of the near future. For my frame of reference I will call this the **KINGDOM REALM of God's Reality.** One of the primary criteria for reaching the destination is to travel and arrive with **eyes open.**

Traveling with open eyes in our KINGDOM REALM of Reality allows us to move from our earliest memories and overlap with our NOW in the present and project into the near future by resetting our consciousness to calibrate to the truth hidden in plain sight that awaits us. Eyes closed brings confusion and offense. Eyes open brings enlightenment and a liberating mind.

You are invited only if you feel you have given yourself permission to be invited and permission to be prepared for this revelation of this moment in time.

Amid the glowing predictions and prophecies for the year 2020 came the unexpected "pandemic of 2020". The public became acutely aware of two glaring questions: How fragile is our health and how fragile is our economy? For both questions the OUR was all encompassing ranging from our self, our family, our neighbors, our community, our state, our country and our world.

Interruption of our normal lifestyle and uncertainty of its return gives us pause to examine our circumstances and our values. Part of feeling comfortable is feeling in control. Likewise, feeling uncomfortable makes us question our control. Questioning can lead us down a myriad of paths. However, the old adage that knowing the right answer is intelligence but knowing the right question is wisdom may provide us a direction to choose.

My path for wisdom questions for the past few decades has been a complimentary blend of curiosity and inspiration. My faith and experience tell me both are spiritual based. Curiosity has encouraged me to study the difference between secular world meanings for abundance versus spiritual realm meanings for abundance for the past two years. On February 2, 2020 (02/02/2020) I received the inspiration to observe, gather stories about, ask questions, interview selected individuals and then chronicle "The Rise of the Abundance Economy".

Therefore, what follows presented in Chapter 1 is a collection of inspired imagination, thoughts, observations and prophetic revelations made as a favored scout into the land occupied by a near future Abundance Economy. The first glimpses are my mind snapshots from the perspective of a scout as he reports back his report. Chapters 2-7 are the foundation I perceive from those invited to collaborate in the Abundance Economy and who confirm their assignments and viewpoints. Chapter 8 introduces Companies and Organizations of early adopters of the Abundance Economy that we will follow and monitor their success in coming years.

The format reflects my personality style of using a combination of picture stories and word pictures to describe my road map of my journey to help fellow travelers to orient themselves and encourage them on their own path to the shared destination, The Abundance Economy. It is definitely not a "5 Easy Steps for Success in the Abundance Economy". It is a journey that we are on separately yet shared together.

So let us begin our journey with imagined illustrations of landmarks of The Rise of the Abundance Economy where we have an Abundance of funds ($7+ Quadrillion), resources, inventions and technology developments utilizing the powers of creative equilibrium, all under the collaborative development and management of legacy thought leaders observing principles under an Awakened Consciousness resulting in a manifested Abundance Economy. Some of my first observations on my journey were to look backward to see forward.

Chapter 1
Personal Experiences, Observations and Revelations 1958-2021

1958-1961
My journey begins in the 4th grade (1958) when I had an art assignment to draw what we thought our house would look like when we grew up. I have a vivid memory of drawing something that looked like a large earthen mound with darkened windows. It was located in a natural, forest setting. This was 20 years before I would be engaged in Earthshelters as a young Professor.

By the 6th grade I was doing book reports on famous architects that were designing houses and buildings that blended with nature.

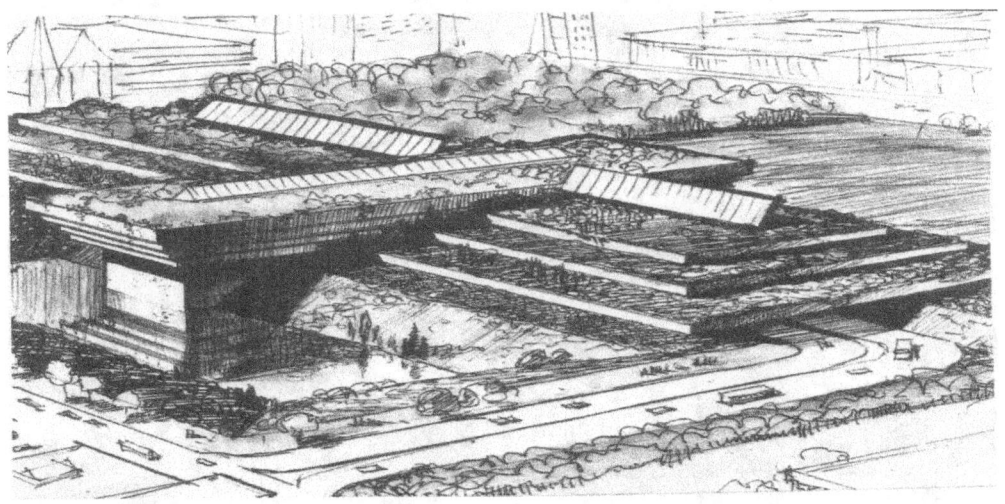

1962

For my 7th grade Science Fair project, I entered a solar project using a Fresnel lens to melt materials to cast into free form panels for construction. Years later there were solar furnaces proposed that would melt desert sands to form fused crystal building materials.

1965-67

In high school I was designing small communities with foundations like circuit boards containing utilities so that modular building units could be plugged in and then changed out because of obsolescence or growing needs.

1968-70

As an undergraduate civil engineering student, I used a material called MM that allowed me to successfully terraform scale communities from indigenous soils. (At the time MM was $100/ounce, ten years later it was $100/gallon. In 1978 we estimated that when it reached $10/gallon it would be feasible for applications. Today MM is $9/gallon.) The response I received from all my teachers and professors was the same "Your ideas are wonderful, but we cannot afford to do that". Waiting for Lack to become Abundance.

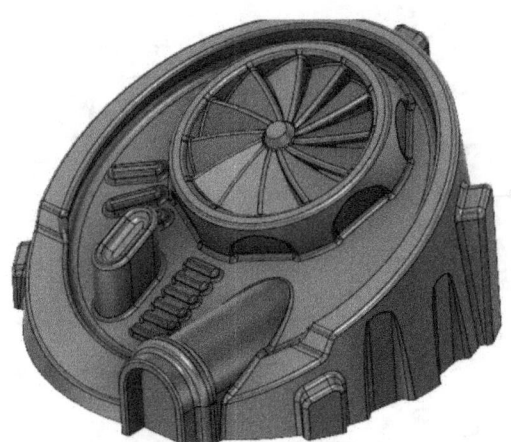

1971

In 1971 I was accepted to work on my PhD in Solar Engineering and using my Master's in City & Urban Planning to propose Solar Powered Terra-Formed Communities. However, the Vietnam War intervened, and I wound up in the US Army Medical Service Corp where I was introduced to the technologies for water testing and treatment for hospitals and base communities. This led me to change my PhD focus after being discharged from the Army to the combined fields of environmental design, engineering and land planning.
As I entered my university teaching and academic career, I added materials science and alternative energy technologies to my areas of interest.

During my twenty-year academic career, I laid the foundation of an international network of inventors, scientists, researchers, developers, business owners, etc. Even today I have been a magnet to attract contacts with those who have been shepherding "disruptive technologies" awaiting their development in the Abundance economy.

Therefore, what is presented for examples for the Abundance Economy are experiences, observations and revelations from myself and from the network of professional relationships I have nurtured over the past 64 years. These examples are meant as catalysts to inspire readers to discover their own landmarks to see the path leading to how the Abundance Economy looks and then how it works. This is a collaborative effort that will grow organically as inspirations are shared.

1976

In 1976 I conceived my first community for active seniors with the premise that college and university alumni would want to return to spend their retirement years to enjoy the academic, athletic and entertainment venues a college community offers.

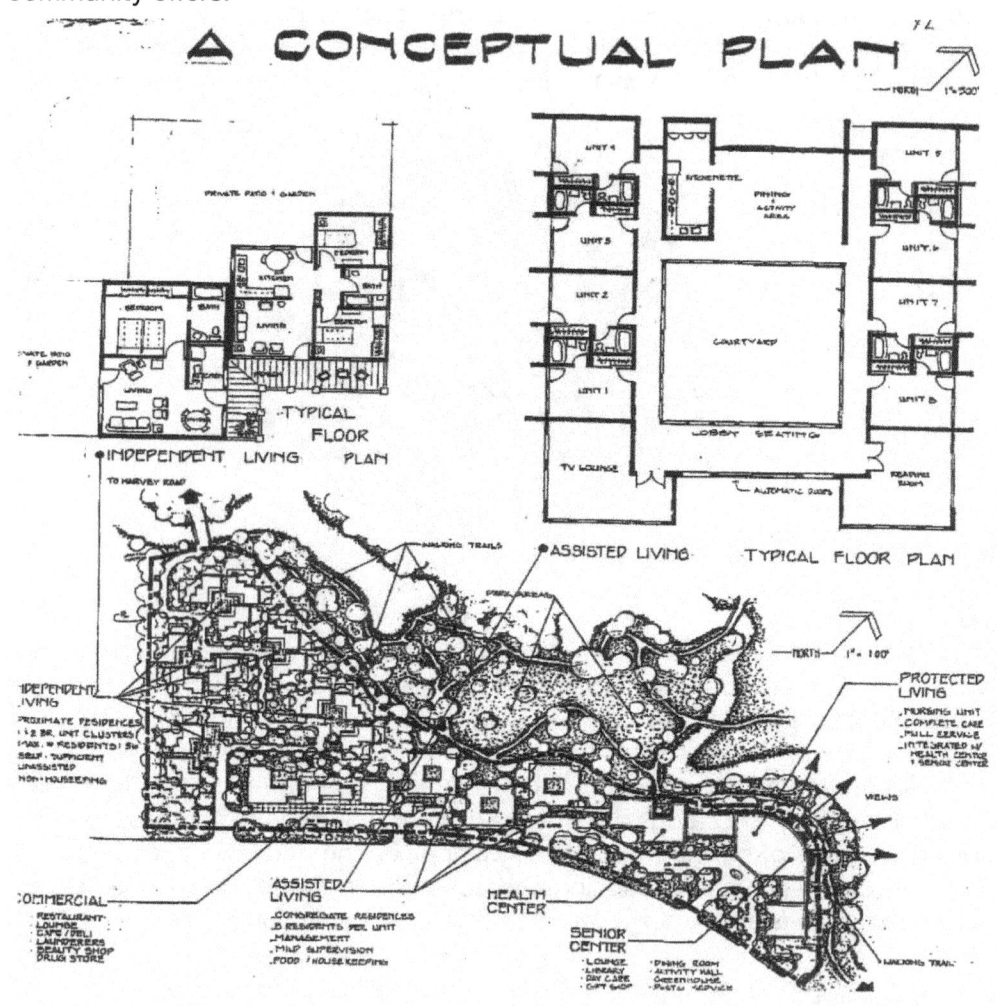

Plans by Gary Sorensen Age 27

1978

Abundance Agricultural Communities May Crease Through Farmlands
If we were to choose a visual model of an Abundance Agricultural Community, we could do well to consider the imagery of the Garden of Eden. Perhaps no other image better illustrates the creative beauty, harmony of nature and sustainable production of life-giving abundance without waste or excess or depletion or contamination of resources. How much did food and water cost in the Garden?

One of the marvelous benefits the Abundance Economy offers is a fresh canvas to start over and not be bound by the limitations of the existing Lack economy. We can look at the entire picture of Abundance from the early stages of our planning process. This is where Open Eyes are important to transition from our current status to see the Abundance image landmarks we can move toward. That is why HOW it looks comes before the HOW it works. To get us thinking here are some of my Earthshelter sketches from 1978 matched with current proposals from industry friends.

1978

Sketches by Gary Sorensen Age 25

2020

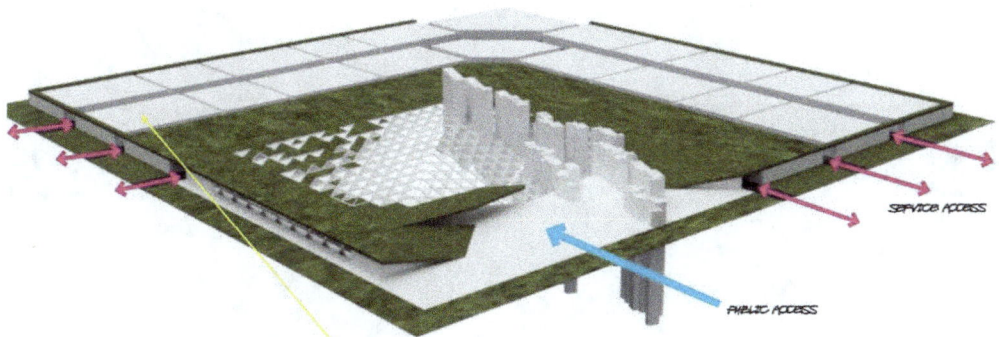

There will be 50 acres of rooftop greenhouses and indoor farming additional lighting. I have been seeking information and looking for qualified farmers to run this space. Below is 40,000,000 lbs. of Atlantic Salmon annual aquaculture

Business Communities May Ribbon Over Prairie Lands

From my design background there is a common expression that says, "you always design with money first". Designing in a Lack economy that is a primary limiting factor. Designing in an Abundance Economy money is only one color on the palette.

1978

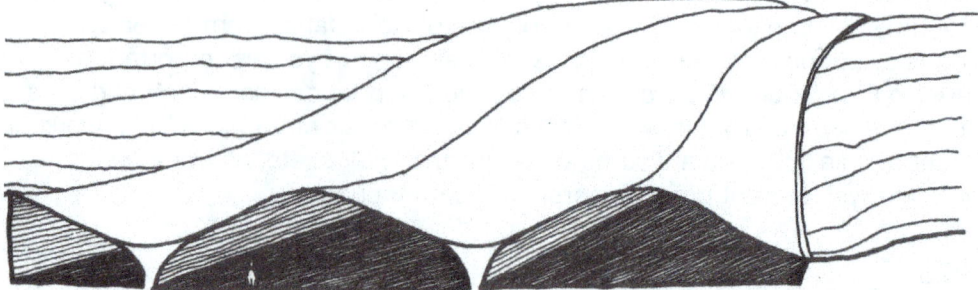

Sketches by Gary Sorensen Age 25

2020

Energy Communities May Perch On Desert Lands
Lack economies want to control energy sources to control power, both generated and political. Legacy collaborators of Abundance Economies may offer universal access to fuel-less power and political freedom and independence.

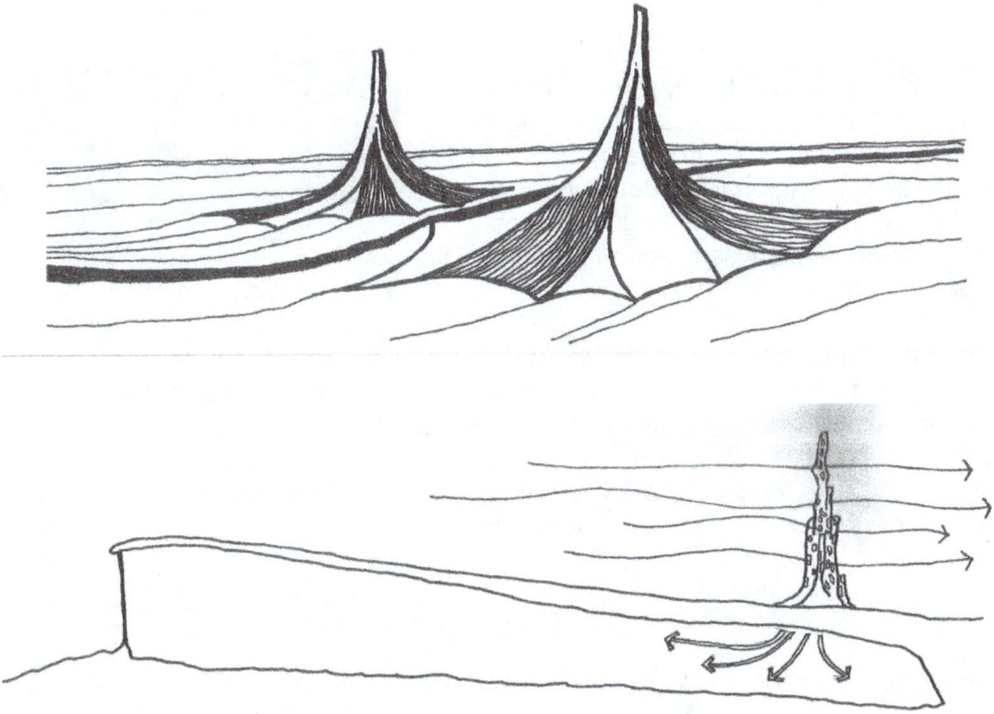

The Rise of the Abundance Economy

1978
Sketches by Gary Sorensen Age 25

2020
Terra-Forming Living Units into Natural Settings

1978-2000

In 1978, going back to my terra-forming curiosity I researched creating building and construction materials from a combination of indigenous materials and agricultural and industrial by-products. In 2000 Reborne Building Materials was formed to offer building materials for housing.

The Abundance of nature offers both the natural building blocks and creative structures for growth and function for living while allowing for adaptive reuse to minimize stagnant growth or obsolescence.

The Abundance Economy also permits us to work where we live and recreate while not destroying the scenic beauty we relish.

Sketches by Gary Sorensen Age 25

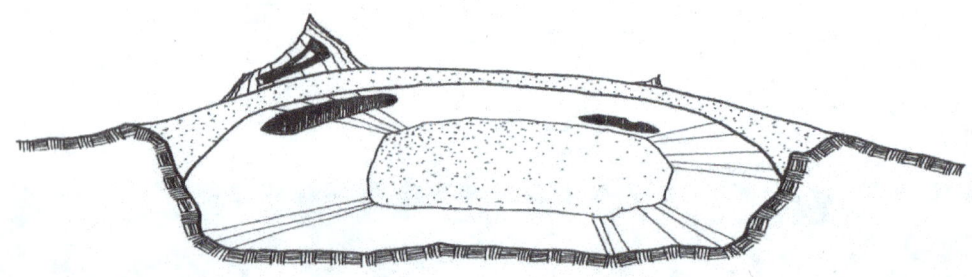

Harnessing Fuel-Less Energy Sources from Nature and Physics

The Abundance Economy will not be powered by limited or geopolitical controlled resources but by a collaboration of legacy innovators with a passion and purpose to empower and share. There are technologies that have been hidden in plain sight awaiting the stewards of the Abundance Economy. Here are some of the technologies from my network of colleagues that I have gathered over the past four decades.

1983-2015

Climate Powered Energy Towers

In 1983 a fellow professor in Israel had a vision of creating an Energy Tower that would use induced warm air cooled by a water mist at the top of a huge cylindrical to cause a downdraft of rushing air that would exit through a circle of fans at the base. Such a tower would provide electricity and condensed pure water for a population of one million. I contacted Professor Dan Zaslavsky in 2010 and travelled to Haifa in 2015 to cement our friendship and discuss a collaboration to bring his tower into reality. Unfortunately, the professor has since passed away, but before doing so gave his blessing to carry on his work to develop Energy Towers on a global scale.

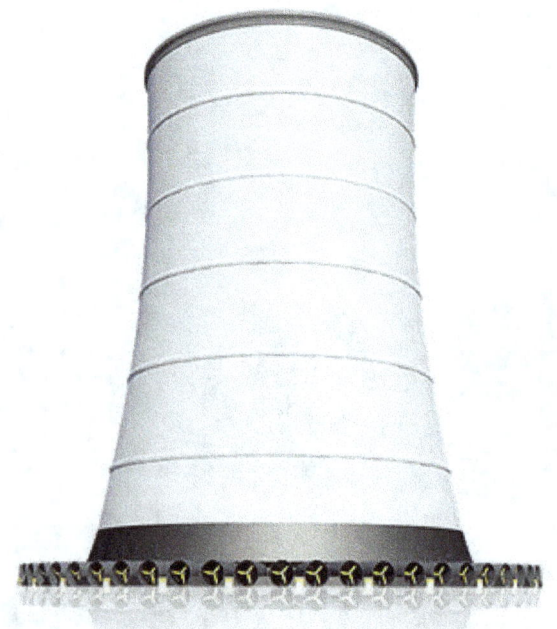

Energy Tower by Professor Dan Zaslavsky

1977-2017

In 2007 I met my entrepreneur friend Joseph Fournier in Texas who has been the steward of a vision for a Pebble Bed Modular Reactor for over 40 years.

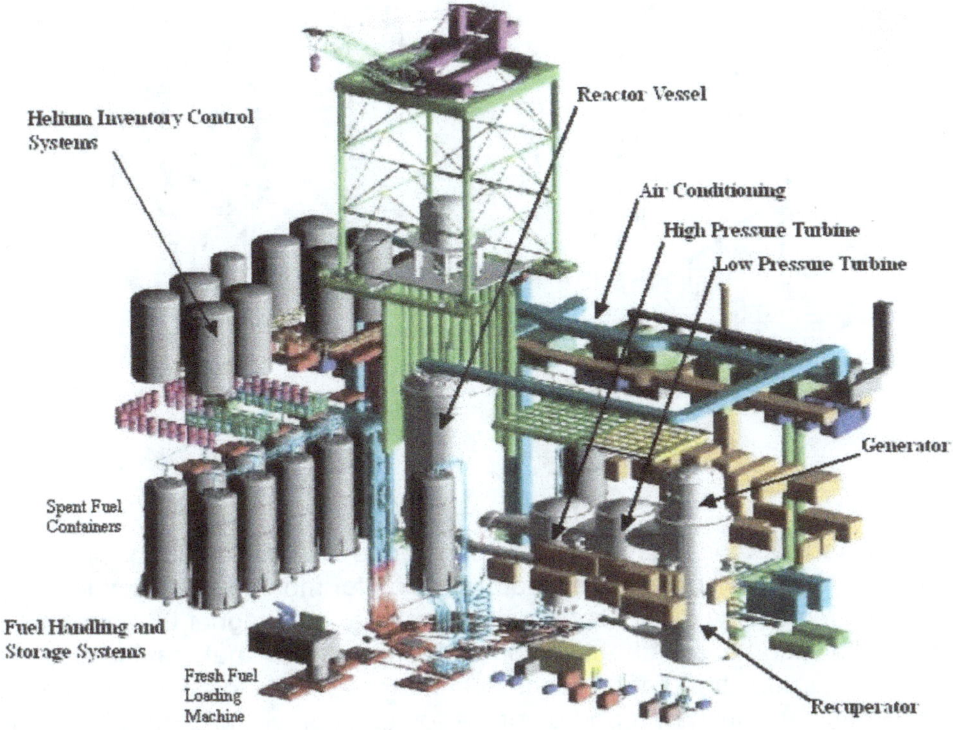

Pebble Bed Modular Reactor by Joseph Fournier

2012

In 1984 I was given the impression of the word **ThermoNeutronics** but it was not until 2012 that I received the revelation of a thermal building technology that conducted heat flow with thermal shunts, nets and circuits.

In 2014 I formed SorenSun Trust, a Solar Energy Collection Technology Company that combined some of the ThermoNeutronics Integrated Thermal Circuits (ITC) technology with a CarbonNanoTube (CNT) for paintable solar shingles and CNT rechargeable CNT battery films from my colleague Dr. Som Mitra at NJIT in New Jersey. The combination allows us to use buildings themselves as solar collectors and balance the heat flow during the seasons.

2012-14

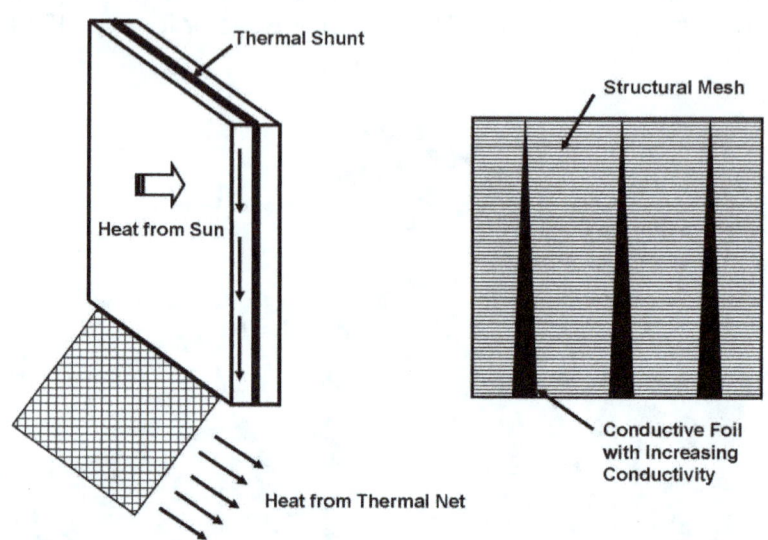

2018

In 2018 I renewed one friendship and began one new friendship, both in California. Both had been a steward of a vision for more than a decade. Michael Kramer saw the potential within a refrigerator magnet that blossomed into the invention of an Attractive Force Magnetic Motor that may be scaled for uses from laptops to home appliances to motor vehicles to power generators. Kurt Grossman saw how a portion of the forces of gravity and buoyancy acting on a sphere can be captured, whether in offshore or on land facilities.

Attractive Force Magnetic Motors

Gravity and Buoyancy Power

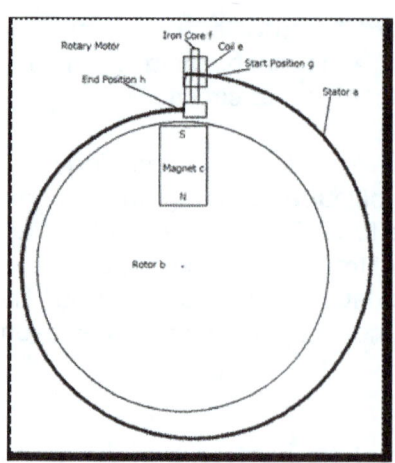
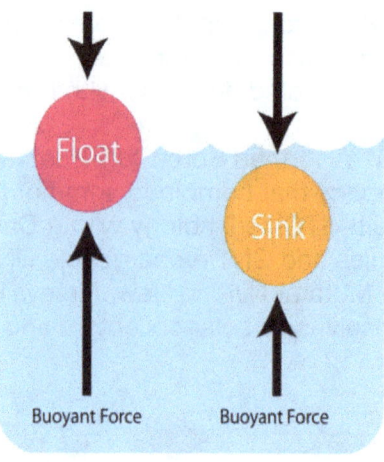

Universal Global Power Generation and Distribution

Likewise, the Abundance Economy will advance the technologies for global power generation, distribution and storage of power to raise the standard and quality of living for all.

Economic timing is often required to move from theory to manifestation of technologies.

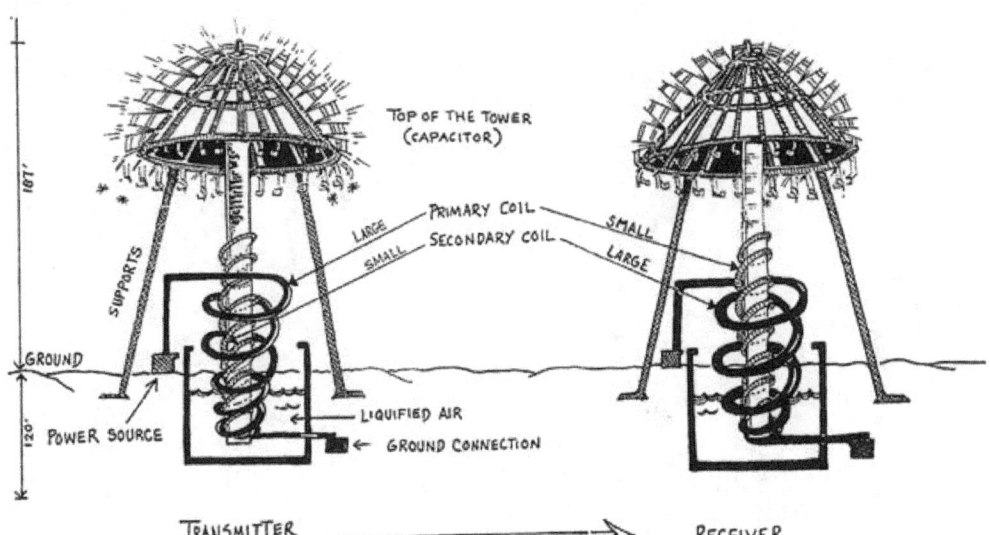

Power Generation Supports the Use of Water Treatment Technologies

2016-2021

The life-giving substance that differentiates the Earth from most planetary bodies is the presence of liquid water. Although we are surrounded by an Abundance of water, one of the primary causes of death and disease even in the 21st century is the lack of safe, clean, accessible and affordable water for drinking, growing healthy plants and providing proper hygiene. A global power and distribution system will permit water to be treated and made available and even recovered and captured from the air in naturally arid climates.

In 2016 our MS Water Group was approached by a physician who represented that a certain natural compound could remove toxic metals such as lead from contaminated waters and from contaminated human and animal bodies. Our MSWG testing confirmed the compounds effectiveness in removing the seven most common metals of concern. Further research is pending to prove the linkage of any of these metals in the body and the development of neurological diseases and conditions. In 2017 we began to explore the effectiveness of the compound to kill viruses in water supplies and in bodies of humans and animals. Again, a national laboratory found that the compound indeed would kill the seven most prevalent viruses. In early 2020 the coronavirus (COVID-19) raised its ugly head. The national laboratory tested the compound and found that it did kill the virus, thus becoming a candidate for a therapeutic treatment that has been safely used for over 100 years. Technologies to remediate contaminated water supplies and remove them from biological life forms awaits the emergence of the Abundance Economy.

Provide Safe, Accessible and Affordable Nutrient Dense Global Food

2019
Below is Abundance Farms LLC that we started in 2019 to use Vertical Aeroponic Towers to grow fresh, safe, affordable and accessible nutrient dense produce year-round with 90% less land and 95% less water consumption. Ironically our Lack economy has created conditions where we have a large part of our population suffering from obesity while being malnourished because of the lack of nutrient dense foods. Globally over 20 million people a year still die from dehydration and starvation. The Abundance Economy can have a major impact on global health by providing Food as Medicine.

Global power generation and transmission can greatly reduce the cost of food production and delivery by encouraging decentralized climate controlled growing facilities and local markets for fresh nutrient dense produce. This will increase the food sovereignty and food security no matter the current geopolitics.

Illustration by Leif Sorensen

Living Space Initiative Mixed Use and Adaptive Reuse Communities

2007-2021

The Living Space Initiative (LSI) project by Reborne Global Trust envisions transforming "empty big box buildings" into living spaces tailored for specific community needs. Rather than just a housing project, LSI adopts the philosophy of the Unified Investment Strategy (UIS) recently adopted by the Center for Social Innovation, Graduate School of Business, Stanford University. This model developed for foundations focuses on creating financial, social, environmental and humanitarian values for measuring the success of a venture.

A mixed-use development of storefront businesses inside the LSI "mall" and outside on pad sites and adjacent properties will provide supporting medical, educational and consumer services not only for the LSI residents but also for the surrounding neighborhood and community.

The objective of this venture is to create a model which can be implemented and/or modified to address the utilization of tens of thousands of strip commercial and big box centers that are vacant, brownfields/greenfields, surplus federal property, closed military bases, underutilized campgrounds, warehouses, large utilitarian structures, rural and historic properties.

The project real estate trust has been established to aid the various tax-exempt corporations that are required to finance, own, operate and maintain the project(s), such as a community land trust (CLT) that is a private, nonprofit organization that buys land and holds it in trust for the benefit of a community. Community Land Trust developments come in a variety of shapes and sizes. They have been used in urban neighborhoods and in rural settings for housing projects.

A CLT could be the perpetual owner of the LSI housing projects developed.

Grow structures for the built environment that compliment nature

1978-2021

Decades ago, my Texas A&M University materials science research included investigating technologies to "grow" our infrastructure and built environment. At the same time Professor Wolf Hilbertz, a colleague at the University of Texas, was experimenting with "growing structures in the ocean". Both of us created viable options that could now be resurrected in the Abundance Economy.

The Abundance Economy will release the imagination of our designers of the sustainable built environment

Take the next step in global transportation and communication

1975-2021

In 1975 I was teaching about where to place(L5) a space colony in geosynchronous orbit where it would stay in place and not fall toward the Earth or toward the moon. This will allow us to harvest asteroids and produce zero gravity solar metals that generate high efficiency solar power to be microwave beamed to Earth.

We have now discovered 3-dimensional radio frequencies that can carry a massive amount of information at very lower power demands, even to rural locations.

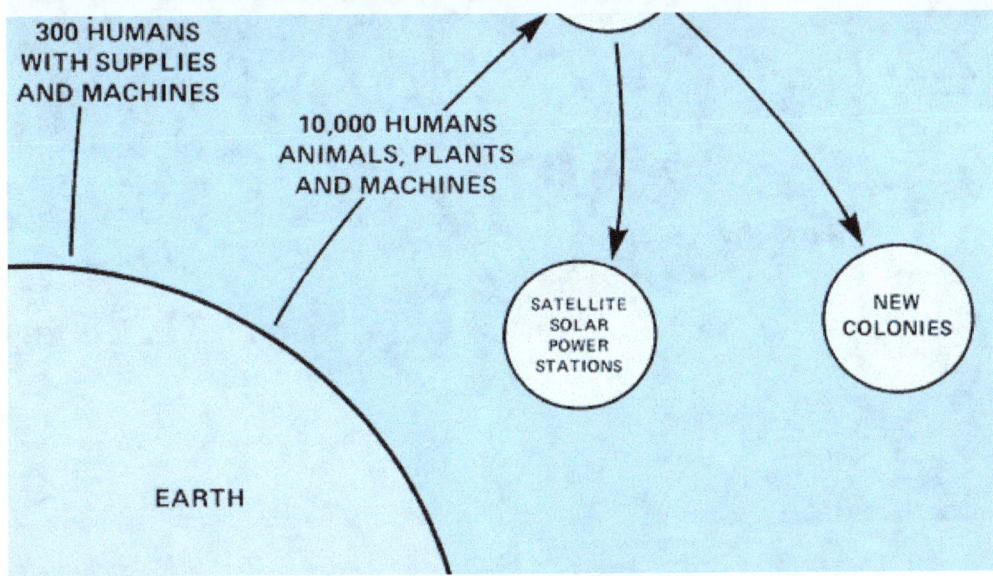

New technology will allow us to have land-based bullet trains achieve speeds similar to commuter jet flights between regional hubs. Reduced travel times will allow us to live where we recreate and give us more ready access to our natural scenic beauty.

Weather Control

2016-2021

Ironically, the same technology that can be used to reduce air resistance can be used to direct major storms and rain showers either away from locations for safety precautions or towards areas of drought in need of precipitation. It cannot generate rain clouds but can steer them for example from offshore to island deserts. Obviously, steering hurricanes and typhoons away from populated areas would reduce loss of life and property damage.

Health, Wellness and Longevity

2003-2021

The average baby born anywhere in the world today in the Lack Economy has over 100 toxins present in their bloodstream. Therefore, the Abundance Economy must produce a healthy and protective environment both before and during life. An Abundance Economy means there will be options to not only provide proper nutrition for growth and sustaining life but also eliminating destructive and destroying environmental contaminants.

New research into genomics, epigenesis and the micro-biome offer protective and corrective measures for healthy immune systems. Biopharmaceuticals and nutraceuticals now offer options to support the natural immune system to maintain and repair the body. Structured water or "perfected" water is not only contaminate free it also provides the effective and desired level of oxygen to the body.

Although the average life expectancy has increased by almost 30 years in the past the century, we have also seen an increase in the time of morbidity (sickness and disease) before death stretches into years and even decades.

Consequently, studies of longevity are beginning to address "Compressed Morbidity" to find people who not only live long lives but also remain healthy and active until they either succumb to natural causes or experience a very brief period (days/weeks) of morbidity.

The Abundance Economy advancements above also have the potential to increase the average healthy life expectancy by as much as 50% (120 years).

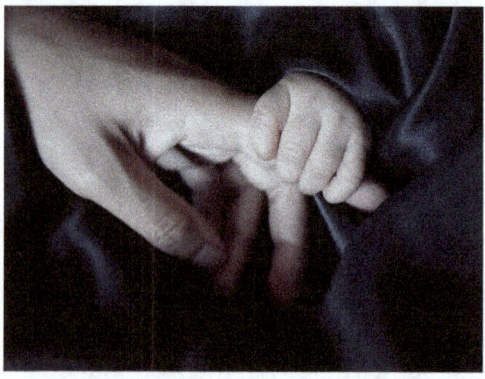

Chapter 2
The Favor Path

Since the beginnings of recorded accumulation of wealth and economic systems of production, distribution and consumption of goods and services we have had the eras dominated and controlled by clans, kings and countries. We are now entering a fourth era of corporate economies with influences and impacts that cross borders and cultural barriers. There are now many multi-national corporations whose GDP or wealth management services far exceed all but the largest national economies. However, this era presents the opportunity to embrace the continued path of controlled competition (Lack Economy) or to enable the path of shared collaboration (Abundance Economy) to flourish.

One might think that from the Chapter 1 technologies and development systems that myself and all my colleagues envisioned would result in all of us being independently wealthy now. Whether for economic timing or funding or scientific advancements or political opposition, ALL of Chapter 1 have been waiting to be released in the Abundance Economy by Legacy Collaborators. Likewise, controllers of vast quantities of accumulated wealth and a collection of individual small investors are being issued an invitation to join as fellow Legacy Collaborators. Collaborative investments in these technologies within the framework of an Abundance economic system can be multiplicative in a way to not only increase the distribution of the return but more importantly positively change the nature of the impact of humans on the Earth.

The collective mind of humanity is beginning to ask, "Is there a better way? Do we have to live in a permanent class system of 'haves and have not'? Does the gap of the richest and poorest need be ever expanding? Can there be a system where all that contribute to success share in the prosperity of success? Can corporations judge the success of their ventures by not only the monetary profit but also by social, environmental and humanitarian values?"

This Review is my subjective and personal presentation of **why** the Abundance Economy works which leads to **how** it works. Rather than sanitize my views into generic discussions and itemized "how to" lists, it is presented within the context of my experiences and value and belief systems. The intent is not to convince you, but orient you as you explore your path to the Abundance Economy.

From my vantage point my observations and perspectives reveal that the structure of the Abundance Economy is different from past eras. To describe what I am seeing I am using my own new terms such as the Favor

Path, Covenant Relationships, Alignment of Assignments, Agreement & Collaboration, Awakening Consciousness, and the Abundance Economy Models.

The Favor Path

Illustration by Leif Sorensen

In March 2016 I was inspired to write an article entitled <u>Grace & Favor in Life & Business</u>. I think it is foundational for what I am now writing about the FAVOR PATH.

Because of my background, as I look at the environment, the earth, the created universe and the Kingdom, I see systems and processes, equilibrium and balance of forces. Today I want to talk to you about the balance of two forces, GRACE and FAVOR in Life and in Business.

Rather than start with fourteen dictionary definitions of GRACE, or as many for FAVOR, I want to begin by planting revelation seeds in you by way of my experiences with GRACE and FAVOR. My experiences are no more important than yours and probably less dramatic than many of your experiences. However, if you are taking notes, I would like you to jot down what experiences are triggered in your memory so that we can collectively explore some revelations.

My story from THEN to NOW begins in April 1916, over a hundred years ago. In a small rural town of North Dakota, USA, a child was born that was two months premature. Even today, two months premature is a concern, but 100 years ago in a small town with no hospital and no critical care unit, there would have been much concern for such a child. Because of GRACE and FAVOR, that child did survive and eventually grew up to be, MY FATHER.

1. First lesson to note is that GRACE and FAVOR can be generational.

When Noah found FAVOR in the eyes of the Lord, that FAVOR extended to his first and second generation. That FAVOR brought 80 years of hard work, ridicule by his neighbors and scoffers, self-doubt and even questioning his FAVOR. What kept him going, not taking offense, not becoming resentful or bitter? GRACE. What protected him from himself? GRACE. How far back in your genealogy do you have to go to see that you are alive today because of GRACE and FAVOR?

Let's move on to the summer of 1951. My family lived in Texas about 250 miles apart from one of my uncle and aunt's family who lived in Oklahoma. In the summer we would often meet at a resort or lake in between our homes so that the four cousins could play. I was 2 1/2 years old and this is my earliest memory.

We were at Lake Texoma at the beach. The lake was roped off for wading and swimming. I was wandering and wading. I was outside the ropes when I stepped into a deep hole. I remember reaching straight up with my arms and my hands but could not reach the surface of the water. I could not breath and just as I was fading out and could not see, a very strong hand grabbed my arm and pulled me out of the water and placed me back in shallow water. I looked around and there was no one there. I saw my family and cousins far away inside the ropes. When they saw me they were wondering how I got out so far from the roped area.

I tried to explain as best as a 2 1/2-year-old could about someone pulling me out of the water, but no one had seen anyone. Looking back now I believe this was my first personal experience with GRACE and FAVOR (from my Guardian Angel). I remember being calm during the entire event and to this day I have a very calm spirit around me (from my Guardian Angel).

Young teenage Joseph found FAVOR in the eyes of his Heavenly Father and his earthly father. I believe both saw Joseph as a gift of visionary FAVOR for his family and nation. But his brother's jealousy only saw competition and favoritism not FAVOR. Joseph found himself placed in a hole by his brothers, but God's GRACE lifted him out of that hole and His FAVOR prevailed to elevate Joseph in Egypt, and His GRACE prevailed to keep him from becoming offended, bitter, resentful and revengeful toward his brothers. When the time came, his position allowed him to save his nation and family from famine.

2. We don't see either the GRACE or FAVOR immediately, and often it appears to us to be the opposite.

In the 4th grade we had an open-ended project to make a model of a house. I had a picture in my mind to make a free-form earthen house that looked like a mound with (solar) lenses for windows and the nearby sidewalk and roadway were all the same material. I made a village that looked like it had been carved out of the ground. I remember explaining that everything was sprayed with a miracle glue to hold everything together. See where this story goes in college.

3. The Lord can implant FAVOR by giving pictures and glimpses and visions, even to the very young.

In the 6th grade I discovered my first hero that was not a sports star. I did a report that included American architect Frank Lloyd Wright, who was probably the most famous architect of the 20th century. A few months later my father had a conference in Wisconsin, so we took our family summer vacation there. We were able to visit Taliesin East, which was the home, office and studio for Wright who had just passed away the previous year. It was my first chance to see the working studio of an architectural genius. In the studio I found out that only 10% of what this man designed was ever built. Then I saw it, one of the unbuilt designs, A VILLAGE THAT LOOKED LIKE IT HAD BEEN CARVED OUT OF THE GROUND. I recognized it from my 4th grade vision.

4. The Lord can link FAVOR together with common visions. His GRACE showed me for the first time in my life that my visions as a 12-year-old might be important.

Two particularly important FAVOR events happened when I was 16 that would shape my career. First, I had begun to think about where I wanted to go to college and what I would study. I had narrowed the choice down to five universities. My first choice had the largest civil engineering department in the free world. Without my knowing it, one of my teachers had recommended me for a special National Science Foundation summer program for science and engineering at this first choice university. There were only 32 slots from our state of Texas. At the graduation service at the end of the program the President of the University happened to be available to present our certificates. In his closing remarks he stated, "You are the type of student we want at our university and if you apply, we will accept you." I did and I was.

I was walking in FAVOR in high school and someone who could grant FAVOR used GRACE to recognize FAVOR in me and placed me into a higher level of FAVOR. Then an authority figure who had GRACE to extend (increase) my FAVOR declared these are the conditions for you to partake of additional FAVOR, and we have seen that you measure up, and because of my authority I can extend to you FAVOR of your first choice of a university.

5. Many people are part of the FAVOR process and they interlink at the appropriate time.

The second event that happened when I was 16 that impacted my later future life happened when I attended a major youth conference of about 10,000 people. The featured speaker was a chemist who had been nominated for the Nobel Prize in Science. He was speaking on the vibration and frequencies of life. At the end of the talk, he asked for questions to be submitted on the cards the ushers handed out. I submitted mine. Later that afternoon I received a response at my hotel room. The note said to meet him for breakfast at the hotel dining room.

When we met the next morning, he began by saying he had spoken to hundreds of thousands of youth and college students the past 20 years and no one had ever asked my question. The question was "Can I meet you for breakfast to discuss your work?" He then began to tell me the secrets of his Nobel work on atomic theory, vibrational mechanics and the frequency of the universe. Those seeds planted would come to fruition 40 years later in my company ThermoNeutronics.

6. Sometimes FAVOR is there for the asking, if you are not intimated.

The last semester of my senior year in college I was selected to work with a new construction material. It was a new "Miracle glue" that could hold shaped earth into any shape, from houses to sidewalks to roadways (my 4th grade project). The only problem is it cost $1000 per gallon. If only it cost less or there was another choice. Stay tuned.

7. Sometimes FAVOR is incremental often separated by years or even decades.

Let's move into my early career after college. See if you see FAVOR in this. I had established a design company and was working in Houston. I was considering moving there and was reviewing the classified ads for an apartment. Right in the middle of the apartment ads was an ad for a teaching position in the department where I had graduated a few years before. I called for an interview and the interviewer was my major professor and he said, "School starts next week, can you start then?" I could and I did; my academic career had begun. A six-month appointment eventually turned into a twenty-year academic career of teaching and doing research at two major universities.

8. FAVOR that you deposit can come back around to reward you with opportunities.

In the classroom I was more of a mentor than a teacher. I would often stop to answer a personal business question and tell the student, "Why don't you try this?" They would come back after the summer and say they tried my suggestion, and it worked. For years I would meet students in various places who would say they remembered the day I gave them a suggestion and they used it in their careers. My teaching and mentoring career has now spanned 40 years and has ranged from first grade students to Ph.D. students.

9. At first I was an unknowing recipient of FAVOR. Later I was becoming a participant in encouraging and passing on FAVOR to others.

In the spring of 1984, I was sitting in my university office preparing for class. My office had a chalk board where I wrote class notes and also tried out ideas. Suddenly the Lord prompted me to go to the board and write the word THERMONEUTRONICS. There was no other revelation at that time, but there were several other revelations over the next 30 years until the formation of ThermoNeutronics LLC in 2014.

10. Sometimes the FAVOR uses one word to imprint FAVOR in your life.
In June 1993 while still at the university, I was invited to a friend's house to hear a "traveling preacher". When I arrived, there were over 60 people in his living room and surrounding rooms listening to this man teaching. When he stopped teaching, he began to call individuals and couples out from the crowd and began to "tell them their future". This was my introduction to personal prophecy. He was almost finished and then he spotted me hiding in a corner. He gave me my first personal prophecy; told me I would be in business and that I will be a minister of GRACE.

I began thinking about turning my research into a business. In September 1994 I met a delegation from Ivanho Power Institute of Russia. The Vice Chancellor I met was the former head of the Soviet Space Agency. I told him of my plans to form a business to turn coal ash into building and construction materials. He told me there are some of the largest coal ash deposits in the world around Moscow and invited me to visit and set up operations. He said he would introduce me to the government, political and business leaders of Russia, then winked and said, "And mostly to the ladies of Moscow".

Major RED FLAG went up in my spirit. The Lord spoke to me quickly about MAN's FAVOR versus HIS FAVOR. I declined the offer.

11. Sometimes FAVOR can prevent you from entering into questionable business relationships.

By Dec 1994 I left the university to start my own business. The Lord had given me the vision for a technology to turn ash into construction materials. I assembled a Christian team with Christian investors. I prayed for FAVOR. I had FAVOR with a major utility and a major bank who joined our team. I was installing our equipment at our new facility and was getting close to opening this visionary business. I prayed for additional FAVOR and I was betrayed by our Christian attorney. I prayed for more FAVOR and both our major utility company and major bank went into merger and could no longer help us. I prayed for FAVOR again and was betrayed by Christian investors. I prayed for more FAVOR once more and we were able to sell the company, but I lost everything I had invested. GRACE helped me endure.
As I continued to pray for FAVOR, I began to cross paths with others with

God given visions who had been betrayed by attorneys or investors or major corporate partners. I developed relationships with them and continued to collect more visions, technologies and relationships.

12. Sometimes the FAVOR path is difficult to follow until we get to the next destination and look back.

In 2012 a friend sent me a YouTube of a professor who was being interviewed on a major TV network morning show about a new solar technology. I immediately recognized it as a solution to a solar vision I had since the 4th grade. I found his email address and sent him a note complimenting him on his technology and said that I would like to meet with him. He returned my email and we set up a meeting. Within 10 minutes we became business friends and began collaborating and did find that we had complementary technologies, not only for solar, but also for desalination of water.

Many months later we were talking about the YouTube interview that brought us together. He revealed to me that from that interview he received 1600 invitations to meet with him but only accepted one, mine. I, of course, asked, "Why me?" He replied, "Because you signed your email with the expression "Live Blessed, Gary" (which I always do). I could see that you are a spiritual man, and I was searching, and I wanted to talk to a spiritual man."

13. We were drawn together not because of my expertise or my experience but because of my FAVOR. Sometimes FAVOR acts like a magnet to attract people that are on the same frequency of FAVOR.

Gradually refined FAVOR helped me to develop water and solar technologies for my existing companies, Marcellus Shale Water Group LLC and ThermoNeutronics LLC.

In 2007 a friend who was approaching retirement age talked to me about Legacy visions and bringing together a collection of visionaries by forming Reborne Global Trust. By October 2014 the Reborne Global Trust Evergreen Fund began organizing. By this time, I could recognize those individuals who had been through the GRACE FAVOR, GRACE FAVOR cycle many times and had been humbled by it. In most cases it took only 5-10 minutes for us to recognize each other and build immediate and strong relationships. We all found that we had networks of visionaries who were bestowed with Godly visions that had been "hidden in plain sight for safekeeping" until the appropriate time and FAVOR relationships were built.

14 .It was confirmed that my FAVOR role is now as a mentor for embryonic visionaries.

From my experience and this gathering of Legacy partners, I have collected some additional thoughts for how you may use GRACE and FAVOR in business. So, let's reflect on our collective memories and seeds of revelation.

15. GRACE and FAVOR are not events but a process that cycles through us.

FAVOR is like a stream where we dip our toes in, go ankle deep or "ask for more FAVOR" and are plunged headfirst into the deep waters and rapid currents. The power of GRACE allows us to survive and then thrive in FAVOR. We can choose to resist or assist.

16. Sometimes we are not the chooser, but we are the chosen, the protected chosen.

17. Sometimes we ride the waves of our ancestors, and sometimes we cut the brush path for our family and nation.

Chapter 3
Covenant Relationships

Portraits of Peter and Severine Sorensen Painted by A. Peterson in 1875

My conscious transition from Christian businessman to Kingdom collaborator began in January 2015 when Dr. Stan Jeffery, Dr. Karl Bandlien and I began to have weekly (Kingdom Congressional International Alliance) KCIA Skype calls as Co-Chairs of a new Healthcare, Science & Technology Commission.
The first thing the Lord directed us to do was to "have no agenda, take our time, get to know each other." After a few weeks Karl had the revelation for us to **"honor** God". Within a few weeks the Lord began to show us visions that He had planted in certain individuals which quickly lead us to travel to Haifa, Israel to bring life to a 30-year-old vision. John Anderson joined us for this trip and on the balcony of the penthouse of the Dan Hotel, the Lord revealed that because we all had **honored** Him, he was going to bring us into **covenant relationship** with Him and with each other.

1. The FAVOR Path may have intersections that lead to invitations to build Covenant Relationships.

The continued building of our covenant relationship required a weekly investment of time commitment to establish a deeper level of trust and a vulnerability to share our weaknesses that were shared and protected by the strengths and experiences of the others.

2. Devoting quality time for fellowship is important for building Covenant Relationships.

All four of us had been in many leadership positions and yet we were learning to grow in humbleness and humility. Rather than jostle for position of importance we were learning to value each other's visions and projects as being as important as our own. Although there were some synergies and having a desire to work together, there was more of a sense of wanting to see each other succeed in our own life's calling. All of us expressed lifelong visions that were yet to be manifested or completed. We recognized in each other that mere FAVOR or opportunity alone was not sufficient for success. We realized that vision quests had not been delayed or postponed, but we had been engaged in a time of preparation for the transition to be powered by the Abundance Economy.

3. Lack speaks of delay, postponement and failure. Abundance speaks of preparation using a concert of Covenant Relationships.

As we grew in our covenant relationships we found that even our FAVOR focus changed to include FAVOR for each other, whether in technical contacts or marketplace introductions or receptive government officials or protection in foreign travel or Abundance investors.

A stronger bond of covenant relationship began to draw us into the power of agreement which is much different than the power of consensus. The discerning power of agreement provides magnification for creative processes but also provides warning signs for disagreements that dissipate power.

4. Covenant Relationships can exponentially increase the impact of FAVOR and the power of agreement.

Our covenant relationships became a template for replication and a magnet for attracting other companies to our sphere of influence. Dr. Karl and his (Transformation Health Network) THN began to attract individuals with projects for hospitals and clinics, medical college, and prototypes for a city of hope ministries. Dr. Stan and his (New Kingdom Global) NKG began to attract individuals for waste to energy, power generation, communications, tourism, transportation, weather control, education and training, sustainable housing and villages, research parks, land restoration, farms and dairies, and specialty hospitals. Likewise, John and his (Global Development Partners) GDP was attracting individuals for infrastructure projects, government relations, nutrition and food production, centers for excellence for manufacturing, energy production, housing and healthcare. My (Reborne Global Trust) RGT began attracting individuals for global education and training, adaptive reuse and affordable housing, energy generation, sustainable food production technology, water and wastewater treatment technology, information technology, recreation and resort developments, modular housing, waste to energy and recycling facilities, modular furniture manufacturing, new magnetic motor technology, and nutraceutical and wellness products. Just as importantly some of our own FAVOR introduced corporate Covenant Relationships to begin to cross pollinate with other FAVOR corporate partners which led to new Abundance Agreements and Collaborations.

5. FAVOR introduced the individuals first who were open and willing to enter into the foundations of COVENANT RELATIONSHIPS before we seriously explored the potential of AGREEMENT and COLLABORATION for projects.

Discernment was used to separate those individuals who might have good and viable ideas but were unwilling to pursue the building of Covenant Relationships first, which also revealed that they preferred to retain control of their vision rather than release themselves into the power of Agreement.

6. Discernment is a safety valve in building Covenant Relationships.

In 2008 the FAVOR of a friend introduced me to Dr. Mark Kauffman of Jubilee Ministries International (JMI) in New Castle, Pennsylvania. We built a friendship that blossomed into a Covenant Relationship with no agenda. About the time I started studying Abundance, Dr. Mark shared his vision for a marketplace university that soon became named Kingdom of Christ University. KCU is presented as a Showcase prototype of a not-for-profit organization to be developed in the Abundance Economy. Because we were on an intersection of the FAVOR path, we began making mutual FAVOR introductions to each other. These FAVOR introductions resulted in the accelerated development of several budding Covenant Relationships.

7. Favor path intersections may act as both a collector and connector of Covenant Relationships.

Here are some examples of Covenant Relationships that have come from FAVOR path intersections:

The Favor introductions by Dr. Mark Kauffman have led to Covenant Relationship connections with individuals leading to Agreement and Collaborations with Kingdom of Christ University, Focus Life Institute, Regulus Energy, Kingdom Green Energy, Information Technology Services, Sovereign Community Outreach and the Allegheny River Retreat Center (ARRC).

As an example, Gary and my wife, Sue were FAVOR introduced to Kevin and Tami Barthen of Franklin, Pennsylvania. Kevin and Tami were simply looking for a property to build a cabin with a front porch where they could sit in their rockers and view the Allegheny River flow by. They found what they felt was an ideal location and began to inquire as to the owner and if they would accept their offer to purchase. What they found was that their potential homestead was part of a 327-acre mountain tract owned by Vision Quest who had developed it as a facility to minister to troubled youth from major cities in the region. The landowner stated that the homestead could not be partitioned off and that to acquire the homestead they would need to purchase the entire mountain tract. In their disappointment they asked the Lord what they should do. The response was, "I want you to purchase this mountain property for MY HOMESTEAD". As they struggled with this decision and finally acted to honor His request and purchased the mountain property. The Lord used His FAVOR and their honor to nurture a Covenant Relationship with Kevin and Tami and implant His vision for His retreat center on His Homestead.

Because of this established Covenant Relationship, the Gary and Sue's FAVOR friendship quickly blossomed into a Covenant Relationship so that we could encourage and support Kevin and Tami's vision for the Allegheny River Retreat Center and for them to encourage and collaborate with our Abundance Farms. Likewise, the FAVOR activated Covenant Relationship continues to bring individuals with skills, services and resources alongside Kevin and Tami for the purpose of bringing Allegheny River Retreat Center into reality.

8. Covenant Relationships are a byproduct of FAVOR and invitation that needs to be acted upon.

Subsequently the Lord revealed that to manifest His visions involves **collaboration** not competition and **agreement** not competition. **Agreement** powered by His **love** releases His **Abundance Economy.**

While the world assigns value based on scarcity, the Lord resources His visions with his collaborators based on His **Abundance.**

Ink Sketches by Gary Sorensen Age 25

Chapter 4
Alignment of Assignments

Stained glass by Sue Sorensen

My first twenty professional years were spent in academic and consulting business. My bachelor's degree is in Civil & Environmental Engineering, my master's is in City, Urban and Environmental Planning and my doctorate is in Architecture and Environmental Design. After my degrees, my university research was in Materials and Environmental Sciences, and my consulting included all the above plus Environmental Health.

Do you see a trend? I like the Environment of God's creation.

In my second twenty years, I left the university and became an Environmental Entrepreneur and businessman. At first it was a poor transition but through experience and hard knocks I became better. I am currently a minor owner in a cutting-edge water treatment company for the most difficult waste waters and a primary owner of a revolutionary solar and heat transfer company.

Now into my third twenty years my focus has changed to that of an Environmental Philanthropist, mentor, and investor in emerging disruptive technologies in four key areas: Energy, Water, Life and Living. My nonprofit Reborne Global Trust is already working with inventors and visionaries whose embryonic technologies could well be valued in the $trillions. My first steps into the Abundance Economy have already resulted in the collaborations of Abundance Farms and Abundance Research Institute.

A major transition for me in this new phase is changing from looking for people to hire me or contract with my company or fund my projects to instead recognizing my life assignment and FAVOR path, meet others who are on the FAVOR path, build Covenant Relationships with them, and THEN explore how we may come into Alignment of our Assignments.

1. Finding proper Alignment of Assignments requires you to know why and where to look and who to look for in your search.
I am now not merely looking for those who can help me succeed at what I want to do. In fact, what I am discovering is that the Abundance Economy is set up to only operate under Abundance business model values.

2. Short cuts will short circuit the Abundance outcomes.

As our KDLA Covenant Relationships matured from 2015-2020 Karl, Stan, John and I discovered that we had an ever-increasing Alignments of Assignments. Although Karl's chief focus and FAVOR was for healthcare, medicine and medical education, all of us found new assignments that aligned or complimented Karl's assignment. The alignment included new energy conversion and power generation systems that could not only support more isolated hospitals and clinics but also provide shared revenue to stabilize and sustain such not for profits. FAVOR brought us new advancements in nutrition and nutraceutical treatments and food growing systems that would provide goods and services for the hospitals and clinics but also provide Alignment of Assignment jobs for the community they serve.

Stan, John and I have complimentary visions for developing embryonic technologies through research to commercialization. Stan has FAVOR with early stages, I have FAVOR with early adopters and John has FAVOR with full commercialization. The Abundance Economy offers us a vehicle to fund and bring to sustainability all three stages.

3. Complimentary visions can be enhanced by the alignment of assignments.

In January 2019 I was standing in line at my local airport to pick up my ticket to fly from Central Pennsylvania to Phoenix, Arizona for meetings. I received a cell phone call from Carter Dye who had found my water treatment company information on the internet. The first thing he said was that he thought his water treatment technology and mine might be compatible and complimentary and that he would like to meet me and show me his technology. Without knowing where I was located, much less where I was going, he told me his offices and research shop was in Phoenix, Arizona. My immediate thoughts were FAVOR path and Alignment of Assignments. As it turned out he was located less than 30 minutes from my destination in Phoenix. On that initial visit we became business friends which within that first year turned into a Covenant Relationship. Although his Carden Water Systems water treatment brought us together initially the resulting Alignment of Assignments of our Agreement and Collaboration was for alternative energy technologies and international Global Housing Partners projects which incorporated my Abundance Farms. The maturing of our Covenant Relationship allowed him to make FAVOR introductions for fellow collaborators for resorts in Baja California in Mexico and advanced nutraceuticals in California.

4. Stewardship of the alignment of assignments not ownership of assignments is a key for seed planting of visions in the Abundance Economy.
In 1989 Tom Meade, a Penn State Mechanical Engineering graduate (BSME '87), having recognized a need for affordable, solid-wood furniture and possessing an insatiable desire to create and innovate, started his company in a 140+ year old barn with a 200 sq ft store. That led to a facility with three buildings with 28,000 sq ft, a 4000 sq ft retail store, multiple websites and products sold nationally and internationally via many channels.

The focus was always to provide innovative, functional furnishings at an affordable price produced with the least environmental impact. Since this paradox didn't exist, it had to be created. Thus, the focus is on an eco-friendly product line using fast growing, highly- sustainable Southern Yellow Pine with virtually no waste by-products (clean sawdust was sold for bedding and wood scraps recycled for burning). The goal was to eventually be 100% energy independent and to set the pace for the industry through product, process and business model innovation - the FIRST Bio Dynamically Integrated Manufacturer in America. However, his vision had experienced a ceiling cap for almost 25 years.

In 2016 Tom and I had a FAVOR introduction because our mutual interest in whole food nutrition. As our Covenant Relationship matured, we found that we shared a mutual interest in environmentally friendly and sustainable designs, his for furniture and furnishings and mine with affordable housing communities (RGT Living Space Initiative). This natural Alignment of Assignments lead to a mutual search to breakthrough vision ceiling caps by making the transition from the Lack Economy to the Abundance Economy. For Tom this meant upgrading his original vision company in 2020 into his Abundance-based Dynamis World Industries.

5. Natural Alignment of Assignments may make smooth transitions into the values of the Abundance Economy.

Painting by Gary Sorensen Age 16

Chapter 5
Agreement and Collaboration

So far my journey has not been too controversial or provocative. That is about to change. The road map from the Lack Economy to the Abundance Economy is more and more drawn in the spiritual context of good and evil and God's intentional creation of past, present and future.

The power of Agreement is not just a matter of consensus or unanimity. The power flows from decision makers being on the same FAVOR path, building Covenant Relationships, coming alongside each other in Alignment of Assignments to support, facilitate, encourage and execute a common God inspired vision. More importantly it is a team decision to come into an Agreement to accept an invitation from God to Collaborate and co-labor with Him in His vision for His people.

1. Agreement with God's vision is more powerful than Agreement with our own vision.

Can the power of Agreement be used without God's invitation? Yes, with limited success in the Lack Economy. God has given free will and limited resources within the Lack Economy for human visionaries to have a measure of limited success for a limited time. The freedom to choose to remain in the Lack Economy will still exist but the Abundance Economy will prevail and displace the Lack Economy.

Can the forces of evil use the power of Agreement? Yes, with the same limited success and time within the Lack Economy. However, as our Awakening Consciousness discovers, God the creator has always intended us to live and operate in His Abundance Economy and the invitation still stands.

Agreement implies coming into agreement with others rather than striving alone. Many of the God inspired technologies revealed in Chapters 1-7 have remained in hibernation because maintaining control for individuals was more important to them than entering into the power of Agreement.

2. The power of Agreement is stronger than the power of control.

As an example, Dr. Dan Zaslavsky, the Israeli professor I met on my FAVOR path had received what he called a God inspired vision for an Energy Tower that would be fueled by cooling warm air at the top of the tower and have it fall which would create a downdraft that would power turbines at the base of the tower as the air was returned to the atmosphere. For almost 30 years he had continued to have FAVOR opportunities because of his government appointed positions and potential covenant relationships he had internationally. On at least 5 occasions he had what seemed to be an ideal opportunity to prove his technology and build his first commercial Energy Tower. However, each project fell apart as he was nearing the finish line. As we became more acquainted, I realized that although he had experienced the primary factors of the Abundance Economy he unfortunately valued the power of his control over the power of Agreement with Covenant Relationships.

But there still could be a good ending to this story. In 2015 when our fledgling Covenant Relationship group of KDLA flew to Haifa, Israel to meet the professor, we had planned on several days of meetings to evaluate his Energy Tower technology. Instead, what happened after the morning session where we were getting to know each other, the professor came to me and said, "I believe you are the group I have been waiting for, and I want to enter into an Agreement with you to help me bring my Energy Tower to life." As a representative of KDLA, John Anderson of GDP did enter into such an Agreement to Collaborate. Although the professor has since passed away, we continue to work with his family's blessings and with one of his chief scientists to carry his vision into the Abundance Economy.

3. The torch of Agreement and Collaboration can be carried from the Lack Economy into the Abundance Economy by declarations of blessings.

Glenn Thomas of Regulus Energy was a FAVOR introduction from Dr. Mark Kauffman. We had a common energy technology background in waste to energy from when my Texas technology partner was consulting with an early adopter tire recycling company that recovered both energy and metals for recycling. As our technology friendship developed into a Covenant Relationship for encouraging each other it turned out our Agreement for Collaboration developed around my network of FAVOR contacts for Regulus Energy. The resulting referrals were for potential clients and Joint Venture projects, but more importantly, introductions to Abundance Legacy Investor Collaborators. Glenn also recognized the power of Agreement in joining our FAVOR together.

4. Do not let your power of Agreement and Collaboration be limited by the obvious.

Perhaps one of the strongest Agreement and Collaborations developed since 2015 was the result of the Covenant Relationship between myself and Dr. Stan Jeffery. It was not built because of proximity, because there are 14-16 time zones difference between Australia and the USA. We only had a narrow window of time each day to chat with each other, so even our connectivity was limited. However, our "frequency" was not limited. Because we were on the same "frequency" we were able to accelerate the pace of development from Covenant Relationship to Agreement and Collaboration.

Although we had somewhat similar backgrounds, we were able to transition from competitors to collaborators. Perhaps our common age also prepared us to be on the Legacy Collaborators "frequency". Rather than merging or morphing our business enterprises we were able to encourage and support each other's NKG and RGT while coming into Agreement and Collaboration to Co-Found the Abundance Research Institute and the New Kingdom Global Treasury.

5. Sharing a common vision along with sharing Abundance values and sharing a frequency communication can accelerate coming into Agreement and forming Collaborations.

Ink Sketches by Gary Sorensen Age 25

Chapter 6
Awakening Consciousness

Painting by Sonya Waters

What is different about this moment of history that would indicate the Abundance Economy is ready to manifest? Although it is difficult to quantify or accurately describe, the clues point toward a collective Awakening Consciousness. I have recently had several conversations with individuals who have given their descriptive perspectives of what they sense or observe about the expressed thought, "There must be a better way." Permit me to offer a collection of conversations for subjective review and comment that express the variety and complexity of the creative climate that is being set for the deployment of the "better way" of the Abundance Economy.

Some of the Conversations come from people who have faced their own mortality recently, others have lost what they thought they controlled, while others availed themselves of the opportunity to "be still" and listen to the voice of their spirit.

Conversations

Abundance Consciousness as told by Tim Stewart

Consciousness is the next frontier for humanity. Consciousness is creation. How? Every intention and spoken word energizes a reality stream. Our reality is created by where we place our consciousness. The realm of scarcity and hardship was designed to agitate our consciousness into demanding equity and justice for all. We had to be brought to a point where human consciousness made a clear choice to reject evil and commit to the highest expressions of love possible. This was essential because we are spiritual beings of free will.

All necessary resources are matched to the frequency of our consciousness. The reason that the realm of scarcity engages with conflict, is to move our conscious awareness *beyond* it. These conflicts all brought a message, but we were trained to fight against them, rather than asking what their message was. All conflicts are angels of love, with a message.

The realm of scarcity has brought humanity to a place of utter exhaustion, screaming that something is horribly wrong: How are we all working so hard and yet people are starving to death? Choosing love and peace in this way, has opened up the revelation about a realm of abundance.

All realms are a state of consciousness. Consider, if we cannot imagine a reality, we can never experience that reality. It is like describing the internet to people in the 1800s, or describing snow to someone who lives in a desert. The new realm of abundance consciousness (which some may call a kingdom age) will feel like an entirely different geography, inasmuch as it is completely foreign to us.

Abundance is defined by some as having enough for today. Abundance is the state of connecting with everything, exactly as we need it. Abundance doesn't need storehouses, other than for logistical purposes, but even this concept still lives within linear thinking. But let's assume there will be a transition period, as we grow into the awareness. Israelites receiving manna from heaven is one example of abundance. Multiplication of loaves and fish to feed thousands of people is another.

Abundance is the fruit of the realm of love. Love isn't a feeling, but an energy flow with a different frequency to what we've known. We are designed to be the expression of this love. In this way, we become the image of God. This realm of love has no boundaries. It is limitless, effectively making it a quantum reality. Things in this realm can never be known, never be measured and remain completely <u>un</u>certain. The moment we know something, we have ended all other possibilities. The moment we measure something, we ended it. The moment we define something, we ended any new potential.

An abundance consciousness does not apply rules or formulae or move into dissatisfaction with what is occurring. Miracles become a thing of the past. Praying for things that are missing becomes a thing of the past. Measuring wealth becomes a thing of the past.

Think of abundance as similar to breathing, where the air and lungs work together without any thought, future planning, agitation or doubt. Remembering that we are creators within a realm being created is an incredible awareness. This is the expression of the magnificent human being.

This new realm is totally foreign to us, and essentially, it will remain that way. This shift to a new consciousness requires a powerful move away from the patterns and language of linear thinking and the experience of scarcity. The patterns of scarcity are very aggressive in luring our focus and inducing fear. For the purposes of this exploration, there are essentially two realms:

>   Love = Abundance
>   Fear = Lack

Abundance can never be realised when our consciousness resides in fear. Fear places us in survival mode. Fear doesn't create, it responds. A consciousness in survival mode only engages with fight or flight instincts, meaning we unwittingly try and *force* things to be how we think they should be. Fear drove us to put money in the bank, so we can avoid the nasty possibilities in our future.

This was fine in our immaturity, but humanity is progressing into spiritual maturity and wisdom. For this reason, perfect love must first drive out all fear. This process removes all impediments that *prevent* our consciousness from residing in love. These impediments are all in our mind. Beliefs, doubts, expectations and entitlements are all quests to *remove* all uncertainty. These things are driving our consciousness *away* from an awareness of the abundance of the love of God. This shift will be traumatic for many. Be patient though, as we've been trained to be fearful about anything that is uncertain, unknown and limitless. This has driven humanity to embrace many belief systems that bring *perceived* certainty and knowledge. The realm of abundance lives beyond all belief.

The shift into an abundance consciousness is not hard work. The transition simply requires that we give permission to merge our consciousness with our Spirit. This is having the mind of Christ. The authority of Christ was the authority to create and we are one with Christ and God, who is love! The truth of this was laid out very simply by Jesus, but our minds prevented us from seeing it.

We are now shifting from the belief in abundance, into the experience of abundance. An abundance consciousness is aware that what we once perceived as away from us, is now a part of us.

An abundance consciousness applies no force to any circumstance, as this disrespects creational energy flows and originates from a fear-based motive. Applying force to people, deals or timeframes shows that we don't yet trust the sensitive and pure nature of the realm of abundance. An abundance consciousness has no need for fear-based memory and understands that planning is usually just a memory projecting forward in order to mitigate against something we are fearful about.

An abundance consciousness is a place of rest. Living in abundance is having radical contentment in all situations. It realizes that our intentions form an intricate relationship with all creation. Away from the toil that surrounds an environment of lack, abundance is radically playful. An abundance consciousness remains in the now moment, totally content with all that is occurring. An abundance consciousness is aware of its interrelationship with all things, seen and unseen. Abundance is a realm of infinite possibilities.

The signature of abundance

The character of a realm of abundance is evidenced by a posture that is thankful for every circumstance. Intrigue, fascination, awe, interest, love, peace, gratefulness, contentment, gladness are the energy signatures that characterize the realm of abundance. These have a unique frequency that has no work to do. It is spiritual stillness. This posture flows from our true identity, as creators who are one with God. Being conscious of our true spiritual identity connects with a frequency that is not connected to the realm of lack and hardship. Conflict and lack characterize the realm of work, as distinct from spiritual rest.

The realm of constant work and lack can be discerned by its energy signature. Why? Because insights and ideas exist in all realms because they are created by magnificent humans. Creation is processed through the realm that consciousness aligns with. The realm of lack engages energy signatures such as importance, significance, urgency and need. They all connect with a belief system that things need to be fixed or improved. They demand that tasks be carried out "in order to" achieve a better world; in order for something to arrive; in order to save someone. This realm will capture any good idea and put it to work, often monetizing it. These targets however, are low frequency judgments of the mind. The tasks required to build this counterfeit 'kingdom' will always vary depending on who is judging the extent of lack. It is not authentic and certainly not abundance.

Lack and manipulation all seemed logical to the linear mind, particularly when shortage and hardship is all that humanity has known. Such thinking is the tainted memory of a judgmental realm that defines the imperfection of everything. It placed our consciousness in the gap away from what we want, and thereby created lack.

Abundance is remembering that we are creators and that we are simply here to express our talents and express the realm of love into the earth. Our expression will do things and complete projects, but not "in order to" achieve anything. Our expression is the face of God. We are the love of God. We are pure talent waiting to be unleashed in whatever way we desire, in that moment. This is rest.

Abundance is understanding that we are the nature of all relationship. Abundance is flowing with whatever is surrounding us now, delighting with all things, in that moment. Abundance never looks for what is missing, but honors what is here.

Abundance celebrates all experiences, whether our mind had previously judged them as good or bad. Everything is our journey of consciousness, from a low frequency realm into a higher frequency realm of abundance. As our consciousness aligns with the frequency of abundance and love, we will experience this realm of awareness.

Transition as told by Sonya Waters

Whether you see it as moving from the Church Age to the Kingdom Age, from the Realm of Perfected Fear to the Realm of Perfected Love, from the Realm of Lack to the Realm of Abundance; you sense that you are leaving something behind so that, together, we can enter into something new.

But here we are…no longer caterpillars and not yet butterflies.

Here in this chrysalis, we are invited to say goodbye to limitless consumption resulting in unsustainable increase. To release mindsets of futility, forcing and pleading. To let go of the laws of limitation, scarcity and competition. To see the futility of spending our strength and resources on survival.

From this safe and enclosed place of transition, we wait patiently in helpless awe…and watch. As a flower's beauty invites its pollinators to feast, watch how desire invites movement and synergy as both flower and pollinator are satisfied at once. Watch how progress and forward motion are not destination-driven but an elevated existence of constant motion. The flight looks indirect but isn't it more compelling than the grounded, straight-line path of survival?

Imagine emerging into a similar realm where need, supply, invention, and creation are in step with our Provider and Creator, all in the right place at the right time. Selah.

Consider the possibility that we are in this chrysalis of transition, being fitted for a realm of Abundance we have not previously been aware of. Perhaps we are being equipped to see this realm that is only visible from a higher perspective. After our transformation, let us see the world as it was in the Garden, the perfection and the evil, our authority stolen and fully restored at the Cross. Let us navigate with increased faith undergirded with a depth of street-smart wisdom purchased through our suffering. Let these new wings carry us to the nations with the synergistic Love of the Father of all who exceeds, surpasses, and transcends our understanding.

Let's not try to leave too quickly. At exactly the right moment, our release will be breathtaking.

The Way Maker Awakening as told by Ross Dickinson

At an early age, I had my first "encounter conversation". A crossroads in my relationship. I was 7. The Maker, as my young mind framed the concept of God, graciously proved to have a personal interest in me by meeting my request for tangible proof: Three times a little chickadee (a small West Coast bird) who was flitting around randomly in the back yard of my youth, moved to precisely the spot I had asked. In this way I was given verification that I was part of a created order under The Makers' control and in active communication with that original source of all I saw.

Influenced by the Greenpeace movement who had their start here in Vancouver Canada, I was awarded recognition at my school for my ideas of utopia in self-sustaining communities. Being an inventor infused with strong corporate skills due to mentorship from my father who presided over the largest forestry company in BC, I began a journey of innovative businesses in 1979 through to present. My focus on sustainable environmental solutions began in earnest when I purchased a US company with a 25 year background in two-stage, controlled air, modular thermal treatment systems in 1989. The vision: make these practical environmental systems the center work-horse to provide power at a reduced cost to cooperative business units in emerging countries in order to establish long term centers of influence where "the way" could be allowed to flourish in abundance.

Life starts in earnest when you loose everything that you think matters. Maturity starts in earnest when those you have trusted were the ones who took it. At one time along my life-continuum, after having lost my house, a few million dollars, all my plant and equipment, with no savings, four dependent children and a very upset wife I decided to take a long walk through the forest. For the sake of brevity I will simply say this: my walk took me off-trail following a small overgrown West Coast jungle stream. After 2 hours I stopped quite exhausted having had to scramble over the small river from log to log that fall across our forest steams from decay or winds. (To this point, my inner focus had been basically a mantra: You are the river of life, I will follow you".) Sitting on a 12 foot stump in the middle of this small river surrounded by dense rainforest, I had my second *encounter conversation*. "My Maker, where am I on my journey with you, and what is next?" I asked through my confusion, heart break, tears and probably some fear. Like a bolt in my consciousness came the answer: "You are half way... keep journeying forward into the unknown to see what I have for you, or turn-around, go back the way you came. If you go back, I understand...You will find the trails you know and can live a secure life like most of the people you see do. It's your choice." "Half way!" I screamed. (I thought I was ready to be a front line environmental missionary extraordinaire!) I was assured I had a long way to go. (Not an easy "encounter".)

So, in 1999 I began again. My first assignment was to step off of the 12 foot high stump, free-fall down through a clump of bushes below to land on whatever awaited me. I protested immediately. "I could get seriously hurt!" So has gone the journey as I continued following the stream, through the overgrown West Coast forest. Towards the end of this segment, say an hour or so later I felt another communication bolt... "It's time to jump off of your logs, make for the river bank.. right there". I protested: "I will get wet, it's too far, those are prickly bushes, that is dense forest...etc. Then I responded: Oh, OK!" To my utter surprise, immediately behind that prickle bush was the terminus of a small trail leading steeply up the bank. Upon reaching the summit, within a few yards on level ground, I stepped out onto a park service road. It led straight out of the woods. The journey contrast was stark. This encounter was my personal, very intimate and uniquely perfect point of revelation. Our maker can and will meet each one of us in unique ways best suited to our own journeys if we seek out the encounters.

I have yet to complete my last climb up the river embankment and step out onto the promised broad road with my water filled boot. That time draws very near. My destiny to take part in advancing the Way through environmental solutions to support sustainable development in an entirely different type of journey path is still ahead. The broad road represents a diametrically different journey path: One that is unencumbered. Instead of wondering what the next step should be, what log to walk along, what stump to climb over, what thicket to scramble through (all the while trying to stay out of the river) my path will be straight.
On solid ground. Direct. Efficient.

At 62, I am equipped and prepared. My wife of 33 years (today) is by my side. My children are grown and independent. God continues to use birds: a few weeks back when I was tired I was told "look up", only to see an entire family of American eagles... the message... "you will soar like these majestic creatures... keep on with your journey." I am surrounded by many other sojourners who likewise share the vision and have been prepared for such a time as this. The Way Maker is in command and control of all time and events.

The future belongs to the Way. I will serve my commander to my last breath (without protests!).

An Awakened Consciousness as told by Roelie Etsebeth

The past few months God has been talking and dealing with me on several subjects. What I have experienced has led me to believe that God is pushing us into a new position. I believe that God wants to release a new authority, power and destiny in our lives. For we need the supernatural to walk into the next phase of what is happening in the world right now.

One of the Bible stories that has spoken to me is the life of Hannah. Although Hannah is barren, she has a wonderful life and a husband who adores her. She finds herself in a place where she can easily fall into complacency even though not everything is perfect in her life. Elkanah, Hannah's husband has another wife Penninah, (her name means Jewel) who has one thing that Hannah does not have, children. So the Bible says she begins to provoke Hannah severely to the point where Hannah becomes bitter. Although she is loved by her husband, she is in a place where she feels like he does not understand her.

So many of us are dwelling in a place of frustration where we lose our hunger for the deeper things of God because we are barren and we lack fruit from our labor. Hannah in her bitterness after speaking to her husband goes to the Temple (the presence of God). There she has even another bad encounter with the High Priest, Eli, the most anointed and highest man in authority of her day in the "Church". He is so out of touch that he thinks she is drunk. But Hannah is not swayed by his ignorance, she is severely provoked with a desperation that is awakened inside of her. She knows that if God does not answer her, she will be miserable forever. She in her desperation makes a profound decision to give back to God what she desires from Him. God needs Hannah to give birth to His plan. She is His co-worker. The Jewel in Hannah's life severely provokes her into fruitfulness. If it were not for a Penninah Hannah would not give birth to Samuel and a Samuel would not have prophesied David into his Kingship and Jesus would not have been out of the seed of David.

Your severe provocation by God's Jewel (the Penninah) in your life is bringing you consciously to a state of being awakened. We often feel frustrated because we are severely provoked by people close to us, maybe even someone we perceive as an enemy. They are God's tool in our life, shaping and pushing us into a desperate place with God. If Hannah was not pushed, she would never have never given Samuel back to the Lord and Samuel would have never grown up in the Temple understanding the ways of God. There would not have been an Eli that would have told him that is God speaking to you. Tell God this is your servant, speak to me for I am listening. Isaiah 60 says "Arise shine for your light has come and the glory of the Lord has risen upon you, yes darkness will arise but over you His Light will Arise!" We have to arise and come into the presence of God. Do not think for a moment that others will understand where you are, what you are going through or have sympathy for your situation. You may be barren right now, but "the children of the desolate (barren) is more than the children of the fruitful." *(Isaiah 54)*

We are not being provoked to fight a world system, but instead to come into a place of desperation where we will seek God's face and His presence so that we can walk into the fruitfulness He has for us. We need to arise from out of our sleep into an awakened awareness of God, His plans, and His purpose for our lives! Press into God, He has great things for you. We are being called to an awareness of Him. Do not focus on what you do not have, focus on God for He is more than what you need!

A Personal Story of Awakening as told by Dr. Dan Nold

We all know that the journey to an Awakening will include prayer, repentance, getting into the Word of God, and asking the Spirit of God to cause us to fall in love with Jesus all over again. But what if it also includes generosity? In Malachi 3:10-12, God is speaking to His people when He says, "Bring the whole tithe into the storehouse, that there may be food in my house. Test me in this," says the Lord Almighty, "and see if I will not throw open the floodgates of heaven and pour out so much blessing that there will not be room enough to store it."

I've been praying this prayer request off and on for 20+ years. "God open the floodgates of heaven and pour out your presence and your power." My first up close personal experience with a move of God something like this was 20+ years ago. I had the opportunity to go to a church conference in Argentina, in the midst of a great season of revival. It was a powerful trip. I remember every time a speaker, a pastor would call people forward for prayer... hundreds would run forward...hungry, so very hungry for more God. In fact, at the evening meetings, they needed security...to keep people in the crowd from hurting others as they tried to get in a better position for a blessing at the altar. I was so convicted by their hunger.

I'll never forget a moment listening to a pastor at the conference praying for the offering. I'm not sure this is what happens in every revival, but he took 43 minutes to pray for the offering. He was praying from Malachi 3. He was calling us to break the spirit of poverty in our lives and our churches by giving away the blessings God had already given us. As I listened I was thinking, "You know we don't really have a spirit of poverty in our church. We're hitting budget. And then God pierced me with a thought that gripped my heart, "You don't have a poverty of finances at Calvary Dan. You have a poverty of souls." And I said, "Yes Lord..."

So I came back to Calvary and started sharing this burden that God had put on my heart. At that time we were about 350 people; compassionate, creative, talented, good relationships, good worship, over all a good church, which in three years had only seen a handful of people begin the life-transforming journey of following Jesus. I shared how God had convicted me that we had been robbing Him, that we needed to live with open hands, that He had blessed us so that we could be a blessing. We needed to break down the walls and get the church out of the building and into our communities. We didn't know it then but we are starting to build a church without walls.

And Calvary responded. We started giving away what we had, in all sorts of way and in the last decade we've seen an outpouring of God's blessing. But with all my heart I believe there is so much more to come. About five years after my trip to Argentina, two pastors were in town doing some training on intercessory prayer and listening to God. My wife, Lynn and I were spending the evening with them in prayer. After a long evening of prayer, one of them said, "Dan I believe God has a message for you." "Okay," I said, "what is it?" He said, "It has something to do with a sword and I think you should know what that means." I thought about it. I asked God and got nothing. Brian then said, "A scripture just came to my mind and with the scripture, the thought, "Ask Dan, what he wants more than anything." I knew right away what it was. It was a Saturday evening and the next day I was speaking on Malachi 3, "Lord open the floodgates of heaven and pour out a blessing that cannot be contained."

Then Brian shared the scripture God had given him. It was Isaiah 64:1-4, "O that you would rend the heavens and come down. The mountains would quake! The nations tremble. Then we would know your name and your fame would grow. When you came down long ago, you did awesome things beyond our highest expectations." After we were done praying I went back to the office. I wasn't done with my sermon. I finished about 2:00am, went home, got out of my car and looked up into the sky. The clouds were red, 2 in the morning but the clouds were red and as I watched they parted and a streak of moon light came through the rendered heavens.

It's a promise that I've hung onto for over 15 years now. I believe that there is more. Paul tells us in Ephesians 3:20-21 that God can do more than we can imagine but what does He want to do? Lately many of us have landed on the vision of seeing the number of Christ-followers in Central PA double by 2030, in the process catalyzing an epic release of leaders. At times I've been tempted to soften those numbers a bit, but I keep sensing God saying, "Don't you dare. Ask me for more." About a year ago, a local pastor that I hadn't talked to for years, asked if we could get together and he told me that God put me on his heart three months prior and he sensed God wanting him to tell me, "You're thinking about doing some big things. God wants you to know that you have a green light for all that's in your heart. He is with you and he favors you, so the visions, dreams, goals, are a 'go.'"

Listen, I'm not a prophet. You don't want me to tell you I know what God's is going to do or how He is going to do it. I can't even envision a box big enough for what God can do. But I do believe He wants us to ask Him for more.

For decades, people in the State College area and beyond have dreamed, some have even prophesied about Beaver Stadium (holds 107,000 people) being filled with God's people. In the past, to be honest, I thought it was unlikely at best, impossible at worst. But lately that stadium comes to my mind and I sense the Spirit say, "that's not even enough, ask me for more."

So here's what I've started praying. Instead of a stadium filled with spiritual fans, spectators there to worship and hear the gospel. I'm praying for a stadium filled with players. 100,000 front-yard missionaries. What is a front-yard missionary? It's someone who is taking seriously Jesus' call to love our neighbors, by first praying for their neighbors by name. Can you imagine if 100,000 Jesus-apprentices in Central PA and beyond were praying for 1 million people by name?

Beaver Stadium filled with Front-Yard Missionaries, Marketplace Ministers, Next-Gen pastors. Missionaries to the Homeless and those in jail and those addicted to opioids and those without a family and those who are so successful that they don't even know why their hearts ache. Central PA afire. I'm asking for more and I'm asking you to join me in asking for more. See here's what I think we need. We need a dream that's small enough to start but big enough to require God's gracious hand upon us. Beaver Stadium filled with front-yard missionaries is big enough to need God and small enough to get started.

So join us.

Pray for an AWAKENING revival in church of your community. Pray that all your neighbors would come to know Jesus and become Jesus-apprentices themselves. Ask God to change your heart so you can have a part in Him changing someone else's heart.

Awakening our Corporate Consciousness as told by Dr. Stan Jeffery

In the mid 2000 God revealed the need to awake the consciousness and discernment of the directors running our global companies and see the reality of God's words to them. In about 2006 God prompted me to start a new initiative to be called boardroom prophets.

The Boardroom apostle is a director or chairman that has God's anointing and is charged to direct the company in the wisdom, ways and strategies that He provides.

The Board Room Prophets was God's idea started in 2006 with a group of Christian business owners and directors who could see the need for support in the board room (from sole directors to corporate boards) for directors and chairpersons.

The need for wisdom and a new consciousness in the Boardroom was obvious from the level of corporate failures and decisions made with worldly information. The Boardroom prophets' vision was to enable our creator God's true wisdom to come to the boardrooms and business strategy throughout the world to strengthen the board's collective consciousness and decisions.

Board Room Prophets was based upon the assumption that "only God knows the future and we don't know". The process was to seek His direction and guidance This was the basis of the whole program. Based upon the promise that the Father hears His children and answers them.

Board Room Prophets was to create opportunities for Directors to receive affirmation and confirmation and confidence that the still small voice (from their consciousness) they usually already hear from can be heard and given authority over the clamour of the noise in the world. In this we seek God's wisdom for each situation to enable us to be victorious in the world and its systems.

The basic need for wisdom based upon God's revelation to the board would enable the company to fulfil all it can be in the current environment and even be abundantly successful. We believed that each Christian in the director's role needs to be equipped to make a difference with the confidence that they have heard from God in their decision making. This then should enable additional resources of God's kingdom abundance for individuals and His churches body of believers..

This process of refinement is done in a supportive and encouraging environment with others who are also seeking guidance. The cooperative nature of the growth of God's wisdom is what forms the body of Christ on earth. What is not always understood is the nature of the battle that is going on all around us. The tactics of the devil need to be exposed to enable us to be wise to the best way forward. The host company has the benefit of additional prayer and encouragement as a result of being the host for the event.

Boardroom Prophets

The breakout groups of three (last stage on the diagram) are to facilitate God to speaking to each of us through the words and pictures from others. This should confirm and support what we may already know. This is to confirm and train us to listen and act on His still small voice and to guide us in the boardroom, management or other ownership meetings. The BRP Prophecy Process **(speaking out under the inspiration and anointing of the Holy Spirit**) can be found in 1 Cor 14.

BOARD ROOM PROPHETS GATHERING

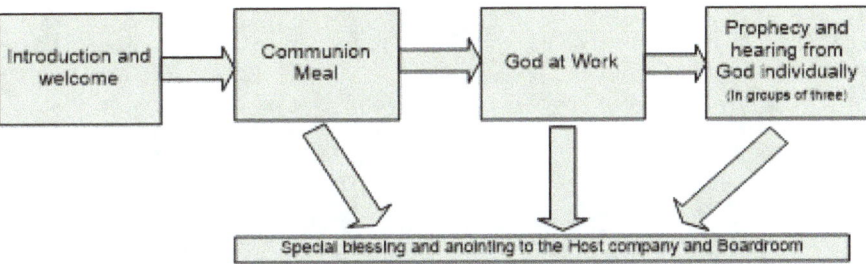

It is quite surprising that everyone is able to prophecy in their own way to each other and that those who had the words and pictures have a strong affirmation in their consciousness and outcomes. This was started with trepidation but ended with great success.

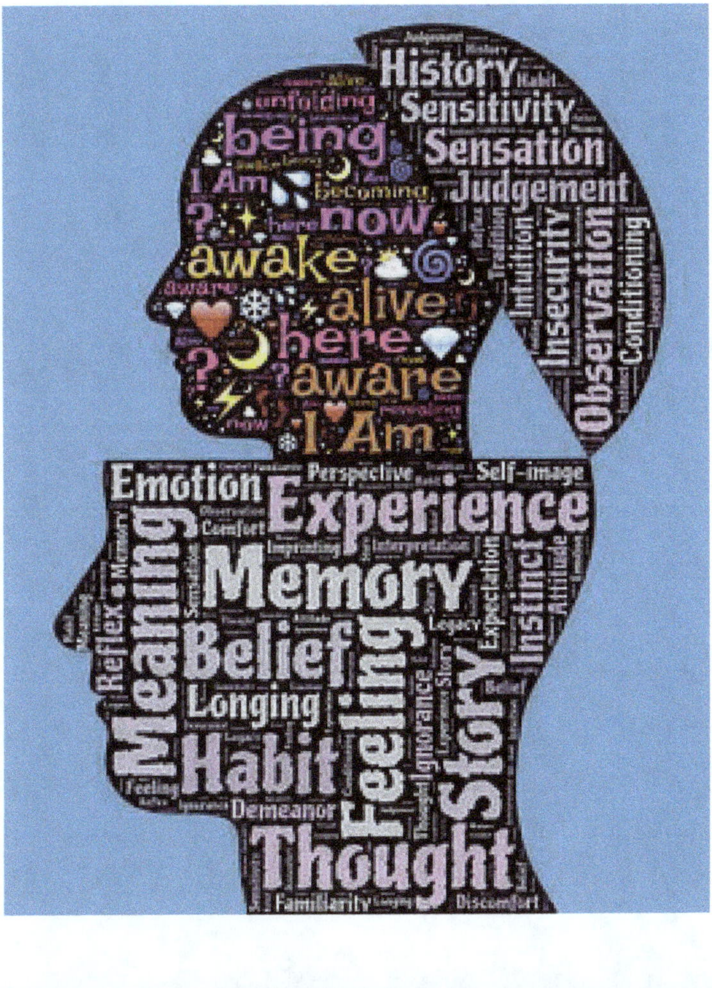

Chapter 7
Abundance Economy Models

Illustration by Leif Sorensen

Now we have examined the Abundance values of FAVOR, Covenant Relationships, Alignment of Assignments, Agreements and Collaborations all within the context and activation by an Awakening Consciousness. Without Awakening, the Abundance Economy will not seem plausible and will remain invisible to most. It is time to get to the central point of the discussion of what may become Abundance Economy Models. There are currently NO active models, but births are coming.

Abundance Economy Models are not structured to simply generate surplus funds and products to meet the Lack needs for water, food, clothing, housing, healthcare, etc. The Lack Economy focuses on what we do not have. Abundance is not negative.

The Abundance Economy is not about creating opportunities for more profitability and surplus but it is about creating opportunities for God's goals for our freedom.

Abundance Economy values are applicable to both small and large businesses. As both the public and the business community see the success in financial, social, environmental and humanitarian Abundance, the template will be replicated. Collaboration success from Abundance values will gradually displace Lack-based competition.

Unlike the present Lack Economy that is fueled by debt and loan obligations, the Abundance Economy is fueled by value assets, seed equity, profit sharing, barter contributions and collaboration. Rather than Pay It Back loans it embraces Pay It Forward sustainable investments.

The Awakening Consciousness reveals that a few Innovators and Early Adopters of the Abundance Economy are beginning to appear. The following are some of the examples of Abundance Economy Models that may become templates.

A. <u>Pay It Forward by Legacy Collaborators</u>

The common match-point for Legacy Collaborators is the shared vision of Legacy Stewardship that lives beyond lifetime achievements and individual lifespans. The "Johnny Appleseed Confidential Concept" of planting seeds for orchards and forests we may never see is a Legacy Stewardship core value. Legacy investors that have been invited into the Abundance process may see their alignment of assignment to compliment the other collaborators. They feel the freedom to use their resources for Legacy Stewardship. Rather than coming into Lack Agreement of debt and loan repayment (Pay It Back) they enter into Abundance Agreement in the creative equilibrium of sustainable investments (Pay It Forward) to perpetuate the Abundance Economy.

As Chapter 8 will illustrate, new Abundance-based companies may use Legacy Funds matched with Abundance Values to organize and operate. An example company may distribute the profit for 30% to ownership, 10% to employees and management, 30% into community benefit and 30% used to Pay It Forward into the development of new Abundance businesses. This could include replication of its own business in other locations or complimentary businesses or sustainable community businesses. HOWEVER, the stipulation is that all Pay It Forward investments must be for Abundance valued endeavors who will be self-sustaining and agree to use a like portion of their profits to Pay It Forward. Thus, the Legacy investor collaborators will eventually see a 30, 60 or 100-fold or more return on their investment rather than just a return of their investment.

The current value of potential Abundance resource capital "hidden in plain sight" by key individuals and collectives of individuals ready to be moved from the Lack Economy to the Abundance Economy is astonishing.

B. <u>Seed Money for Equity</u>

Within the revenue cycle of the Lack Economy are the seeds to be replanted into the Abundance Economy. The vision for Seed Money for Equity is to develop an evergreen (self-sustaining) fund based on secured and donated assets to finance "seed money for equity" that results in the commercialization and deployment of sustainable and "disruptive" technologies and projects and corporations. This will produce viable global economic, humanitarian, social and environmental stewardship models that in replication may serve with positive effects for employment and improved quality of life in developed and emerging countries.

Open Collaboration is defining and creating opportunities, as well as sharing the rewards and reinvesting the abundance while safeguarding IP and technology transfer.

Seed Money for Equity considers Global Impact as part of its vision, not just technology changing but life enhancing and sometimes lifesaving impact. Solutions are sought that have macro and micro scale applications. Access for all to the technologies is an essential criterion for Global Impact.

In Chapter 8 there are Abundance examples such as the RGT Evergreen Fund and the Abundance Research Institute that employ the Seed Money for Equity Collaboration. It operates within the same parameters of the Pay It Forward Legacy Collaborators with the exception that the above entities assist in identifying, vetting and funding candidates for Abundance funding and operation.

Whereas the Pay It Forward Legacy Collaborators focus on companies using existing and proven technologies and systems, the Seed Money for Equity entities invest in bringing visions from conception through research and development to commercialization launch stage. In addition to Seed Money the Abundance candidates must be in Agreement with Abundance values and accept counsel and guidance and oversight during their progress.

The Abundance companies may use equity portions similar to the 30:30:30:10 ratios with future options to repurchase or by back equity as long as the Pay It Forward plan continues as agreed to. Others may have successful ratios operating at 25:25:25:25 or 40:30:20:10 or even 40:40:10:10. The Seed Money for Equity entities may also option to sell all or a portion of their equity in the future and use such proceeds to add to their evergreen funds for financing Abundance companies.

It is important that all equity collaborators remain committed to the Agreement of the Collaboration and reserve the right to purchase the equity of any other member and not break the collaboration to allow anyone not committed to the Agreement and its Abundance values to enter the Collaboration. The Seed Money for Equity entities will have a Stewardship role in the continuity success of the Collaboration.

C. Profit Sharing Collaborations
A variation of the Seed Money for Equity model is the Seed Money for Profit Sharing model. There may be circumstances where specific countries do not

allow the Equity model and require all profits to be dispersed each year. The same may be true of some Not For Profit business and enterprises. The intent for all models is to promote sharing of Abundance values and sustainable prosperity.

D. Community (Hybrid) Corporations

Several of our Abundance Collaborators desire to form what we are calling Community Corporations which act as a hybrid with characteristics of both sustaining profit generating entities and community serving entities. Such hybrids may use their products or services instead of cash profits for providing food, water, housing, healthcare and education for their community mission. They still provide well-paying jobs and reward sharing for management and employees while demonstrating the ability to Pay It Forward with products and services to the community and support new Pay It Forward entities.

E. Redemptive Business

The Redemptive Business model is centered on the Biblical worldview that our God desires to bring choice based economic freedom to the nations through the business sphere of influence in order to enable people to build His Kingdom on earth. Included in this is the requirement of good stewardship of the planet first mentioned in Genesis. Applying God-inspired technologies will help countries, provide strong economic benefits to the nation including eventual local majority ownership, and partner with the local communities through benevolent giving programs.

F. Inventors in Residence Program

Incubate promising technologies by hosting inventors through "Inventor in residence program". In order to qualify for this program, an invention must be able to transform the lives of millions of people.

G. Cooperative Model

This type of structure is well known in the USA and Canada. Every employee in this model is an owner, therefore at the outset, the model empowers each worker with a voice in the cooperative.

Pay-it-Inward

Abundance results as all members are rewarded equally as the goals of the Cooperative are met through a profit share and retirement fund.

Pay-it-Forward

As new cooperatives are established and profitable, they pay forward by contributing to the new cooperative by sharing risk through the pledging of assets and staff resources for training.

Pay-it-Backwards
As recognition that the initial conception, finance and efforts made without thought of rewards but made in faith, in total attitude of risk, with the knowledge that the Maker who is the Master of Multiplication is just doing what is natural as we operate in an Abundance attitude. Abundance comes from setting up a cooperative that serves the community by ridding it of a broken economic system that surrounds the cooperative. Paid Forward to it by benefactors, the profit is significant. The beneficiary is the Cooperative and each individual that is an employee Member. Abundance in this model comes from the opportunities that will result from Membership collaboration.

H. Flow of Funds Model
The simple basis for the Flow of Funds Model is to make sure that everyone who participates receives tangible value. The 'flow' of money, rather than the accumulation of funds in storehouses, is what fuels economic momentum, with less dependency on credit. The sharing economy built on this mindset will produce regular small profits from each transaction. This abundance model focusing on the flow of funds is based on a simple method of using existing and well-established systems used in real estate and business that don't require complicated strategies or regulatory approval. The model aims to help reinforce abundance thinking for everyone in the community, at every level as we strive to increase the wealth of others and ourselves so that the community prospers as we help those most in need.

CONVERSATIONS

Abundance Economy Technologies as told by Michael Kramer

Currently, the **greed driven multi-trillion dollar per year monopoly of carbon-based fuels** and energy has made it **unlikely that low cost, clean alternative energy solutions will make a substantive impact** on humanity **for the foreseeable future. Hundreds of trillions of dollars will be required to facilitate the R&D and subsequent changes** to worldwide infrastructure and governmental regulation in order to change the tides in the direction of low cost, clean and abundant energy for all.

The conversation needs to focus on access to cheap abundant energy as basic Human Right. It is incredible that in the technological age we currently live, **billions of people are still living without the electricity** that is required for lighting, internet connectivity, farming, refrigeration, transportation, clean water, sewage treatment, and other basic necessities of life!

We, humanity, must do better!

Technologies and technologists exist today that can achieve this end. Since the late 1800's, **technologies and people have been suppressed and marginalized, eliminated by the people that run the carbon economy** and who profit from staying in control. This even happened to Nikola Tesla, one of humanities greatest visionaries and inventors. He was marginalized by his then benefactor, J.P. Morgan when it was disclosed that Tesla wanted to provide free energy from his Wardenclyffe transmission tower.

en.wikipedia.org/wiki/Wardenclyffe_Tower

A **paradigm shift** must occur that will **empower** the people waiting in the wings to effectuate the required change. Huge sustained sums of money will be required to accomplish this **new vision of low cost, abundant energy** for all as a basic **Human Right**.

The latest focus on **climate change** is laudable, but it **misses the point** and is the wrong focus **as it leaves billions of people behind**, not enjoying the benefits of low cost clean energy. Although it makes perfect sense to have clean energy and a clean atmosphere, we must focus on increasing worldwide human productivity and the **lifting of billions of people out of poverty** to a **new levels of productivity and quality of life**.

The **Kingdom Vision** must include providing **low cost, clean energy to all as a Basic Human Right**, so that we all shall prosper.

Abundance Cooperatives as told by Ross Dickinson

A chosen (predestined) people were set apart to demonstrate a society mirroring heaven. Framework and routines were provided which were designed to encourage independent family units with linkage to tribes or genetic pools to individually forgive, provide restitution and celebrate jubilee years or reset. These basic frameworks are still valid, but now enhanced by revelation. We are existing temporally in an advanced dispensation where GRACE has been hung out for all to see. Where "service" is given definition.

Fundamental to any form of enduring organization we envision will be a "service" founded on selflessness. Other words for GRACE. To imagine an organizational structure that relies on FAVOR, that is, the acceptance of or revelation of GRACE at the individual level; which fails to account for SIN is a fallacy and naïve in this dispensation.

To put our hope in a justice system conceived by the created is to operate out of FAVOR / GRACE. How we may choose to structure our Agreement and Covenant is in a written context that sets forth a constitution specific to the "service" mission. But to imagine it as a mechanism to be arbitrated by a court of man is a fallacy.

We are told of acts, in Acts, where a community of quantum beings (beings able to think and communicate faster than the speed of light) who: Agreeing that a new Kingdom had been revealed by an act of GRACE; decided to commit themselves to a new form of living arrangement. Each worked in their own way, with skills and resources they had as a means of fulfilling the original intent of the given Framework for the chosen people.

To the degree possible, and as Wisdom directs, our methods of organization will find FAVOR as they align with the original Framework and are designed to be tested and remedied by that Framework as opposed to a judicial framework constructed by fallen beings. To that end: Those who participate in the organization at any level of control ought to be well schooled in the mysteries of GRACE.

My journey has led me to study cooperatives as a possible template for organization with the constitution being founded in selflessness commitments by the members for adjudication by a body of elders who have publicly practiced GRACE and FAVOR and are yet separate of the organization (the Church). This is Accountability. Leaders of the organization ought to willingly agree to be accountable to a separate group in the case where internal GRACE fails: That is where even after numerous meetings
one on one, followed by witnessed meetings resolution is unattainable.

Abundance in Business as told by Dr. Stan Jeffery

I have asked God a number of times what a kingdom abundance person would look like to others in the kingdom and even those outside God's kingdom. The scripture clearly says that you will know them by their love for one another.

This is important particularly in the financial investment in each other's businesses. How do you see the love manifest? How does the love for one another appear?

A correlated aspect in the investment area is that God will not allow His funds to be used to enhance Satan's kingdom. He is a jealous God and doesn't want His resources building up the god of this world and deceiving even more people.

For these reasons, we need to look for abundance kings who are not wholly focused on their own project/missions so much that it becomes their god. But are assisting other abundance kings with their missions also. The love can be manifest in the giving to others ahead of yourself and then you will find there is enough to go around if God is in charge.

Kingdom Workplace Model

The following is a quick but not exhaustive identification of ideas that may help us to think about some of the kingdom abundance issues in His kingdom abundance business of the future.

1. The currency of the Abundance Kingdom is Love before money (sounds a bit puerile, however it is the truth and we had better find the ways to implement it).
2. Replace capital with people (employ as many people as possible!).
3. Cooperation before competition (start a new paradigm of trusting each other as the body of believers).
4. Develop simple life (back to the garden) basics models (return the land and resources back where possible to their created state).
5. Maximise creation, minimise capital (allow everyone the opportunity to create) each person has infinite worth in God's Abundance Economy.
6. Physical skill above virtual skills (honour and reward artisans and trades people).
7. Purchase and make lasting products that are maintainable and repairable.
8. The joy and fun of helping and investing in one another.
9. Commit to buying each other's product.
10. Supply chain development to reduce dependence on external forces and policies.

11. Own internal Kingdom Abundance banking and or goods trading system.
12. Value and reward honour and integrity. Build a Kingdom Abundance structure and celebrate good fruit.
13. Not simply investment, but Kingdom Abundance growth and returns.
14. Use of natural products and medicines instead of overpriced artificial products.
15. Enjoy our life with our creator and not in the company of the devil's toys and systems.
16. Manifest Abundance and generosity to each other.
17. Do not compromise if you will be fighting against the creator.

This will require substantial change in the current world economic system which is based upon allocation of scarce resources and its constant effort to create them, even artificially (i.e. bitcoin etc).

Clearly this is a difficult task in the current world, however, we are talking about a new world/wineskin here on earth The foundation is based upon the Abundance Kingdompreneur.

Abundance Truths as told by Brigette Marx

I am so blessed to have the privilege to read through this book and I feel the Fathers heartbeat in this module.

There is so many Biblical truths built into this module and one of them that comes to mind is the Church of Acts and how everyone brought and shared in everything they had and no one had any lack.

The Lord has also impressed the vision of building and securing for 1000 generations to come and I believe this module plays such an integral part in doing so.

What you are building also makes me think of an Empire as you are bringing many "kingdoms" together to collaborate under one corporate vision even though there is liberty for multiple visions to come into existence and to be safeguarded for the generations to come. Giving all the right to exist according to Heavens agendas and mandates.

From a spiritual point of view I may suggest a few strategic building blocks and plans to put in place to safeguard and advance this vision from Heaven to earth and I hope to be of assistance within my respective call, anointing, giftings and experience.

Furthermore, it is my belief that our success will be in our unity because the most dangerous position to hold is a position of isolation.

The Abundance Economy and Credit as told by Gary Lovelace

Credit will not be needed as a standard operating practice in the Abundance Economy.

This does not mean that there may be occasional times of borrowing minimal amounts for very short-term purposes. In these situations interest will be moderate/minimal and penalties for late or nonpayment will not incapacitate the borrower. They will be administered with justness, fairness, and a golden rule guideline. Therefore, forbearance, forgiveness, and gifting may be the end result depending upon the Holy Spirit's guidance.

When there is a project need for capital beyond the available cash on hand, the transaction will be crafted more as a partnership/investment than traditional credit. That way all parties benefit. If those needing the capital cannot fulfill their responsibilities in the transaction then their position can be purchased, or modified. These adjustments must likewise be administered with the golden rule mentality and fairness.

This approach to an economic structure also minimizes the opportunity for people to purchase beyond their needs and ability to repay. Instead, it will promote savings, and patience, until sufficient cash is available to purchase in needs and assets. It will cause people to more often ask the question "do I really need this item now"? Or cause them to be more efficient and creative, how they may be able to use their skills and God-given talents to make additional money.

This approach will also minimize the marketplace opportunity for those of greed to prey upon the needs of those less fortunate for exorbitant interest rates.

Our present economic system both personal, business and government has created an environment whereby credit ultimately destroys the borrower. This is as a result of credit based inflation, or the creation of fiat currency with no asset backing.

This is certainly not the basis for an Abundance Economy.

Ideally, the Abundance Economy has no need for credit, because those with the abundance will be providing capital investment, not credit for the continued growth of the system, for the benefit of all.

Those needing more money will be dependent upon God's abundance operating in their lives as they provide their input into the Abundance Economy. This system stands ready to be blessed by God because of the caring for one another principles that it is based upon.

Chapter 8
Abundance Companies and Organizations

There are some current companies that practice some of the Abundance essentials from Chapters 2-7 by chance but only a few that are intentionally pursuing the principles purposely to develop and grow in the Abundance Economy. The Abundance Companies and Organizations presented here are some examples of early adopters, both small and big, that serve as both templates and forerunners. However, they are not the only models or templates. As more individuals Awaken there will be more expressions revealed for templates for Abundance Economy success.

Ironically, the Innovators and Early Adopters may be first represented by the Legacy Collaborators who have already experienced a lifetime of Lack Economy success and are looking for "the better way" as a last hurrah.

What is sure is that wherever you are when you accept the FAVOR invitation to move from Lack to Abundance, you will start where you are. It is like when a new country is formed, all of its original citizens are foreigners.

Some of the Abundance Company and Organization examples are starting from scratch, but most are starting again, starting over and making a transition. Perhaps some of the most difficult transitions will be for charities and ministries who have operated almost exclusively in the Lack Economy. It may be difficult for them to take that first step of Awakening and Awareness. They have long walked the fine line between fundraising and mission, often with the former limiting the latter.

Being an Abundance Company does not mean they have crossed the finish line but they are on the learning curve pursuing Abundance. For those in transition from existing Lack-based to Abundance-based the picture is still a bit cloudy.

Bear in mind that the perspectives of both the Innovators and Early Adopters and Observers of the transitions are still looking to find new landmarks for reference in the Abundance Economy. The current GPS road map presented here is subject to future declarations of "recalculating".

The Abundance Companies will be identified by Name and Founders/Owners with accompanied narrative of why and how the company was formed and the observations of the reality of incorporating the Abundance Economy values and principles into their structure and success of the venture. The Company abstract summaries and observations of Abundance values and principles are offered by the founders and owners.

Abundance Farms LLC
Founded by Dr. Gary and Sue Sorensen 2019

Abundance Farms LLC, www.abundancefarms.live facilitates the development of residential, community and commercial Farms and e-Markets by using vertical aeroponic technology to grow nutrient dense locally grown living produce year-round that is safe from unhealthy pesticides and fertilizers while efficiently using 90% less land and 95% less water.

Abundance Farms and e-Markets can be developed in urban food deserts or remote rural locations, or in harsh winter or summer climates, or in areas of water and soil scarcity.

Abundance Farms will help assemble teams of property owners, grower/farmers, marketers, distributors, retailers and investors to develop indoor, greenhouse or outdoor and seasonal farms.

Our Abundance Farms works with the Commercial Tower Farm consulting team which is comprised of professional growers, horticulturists, aeroponic experts, greenhouse engineers, architects, and LEED AP specialists. The team is led by Tower Garden® developer Tim Blank, a hydroponics expert, global farm developer, and 12-year hydroponics veteran of the Walt Disney World Company.

Abundance Farms is also establishing Abundance Farms e-Markets to offer retail sales and e-commerce sales. These markets can be in conjunction with the wholesale farms or as separate stand-alone markets. The Abundance Farms e-Markets may also have their own smaller scale indoor or outdoor farms for support.

There will be partnership and investment opportunities for equity positions and revenue sharing in both individual Abundance Farms and Abundance Farms e-Markets. There will also be management opportunities for Abundance Farms Regional Directors.

12 advantages of vertical aeroponics with Abundance Farms

Agriculture is a thriving industry — new farming businesses are sprouting up all over the world. Abundance Farms can help yours be successful in the following ways:

1). Farm almost anywhere.
You can grow food in a variety of unlikely places — indoors and out — thanks to the unique design of our vertical aeroponic growing systems. To get started, all you really need is about 200 square feet, a clean water source, electrical outlet, and sunlight (or grow lights).

2). Get farm financing and cut startup costs by 75%.
Starting even a small farm usually requires a large pocketbook. But low interest financing through Tower Farms makes urban agriculture more accessible. In fact, you can get growing with a down payment of only 25%.

3). Maximize yields in minimal space with up to 250,000 plants per acre.
A single tower unit takes up less than 6 sq ft. and uses stackable sections that can hold four plants each. (So, an 11 section-tall unit accommodates 44 plants.) That means you can produce up to 10x more food than a conventional farm of the same size — without paying for extra land.

4). Deliver 30% more product to market, 3x faster.
The aeroponic growing process produces up to 30% greater yields and is 3x faster compared to traditional farming methods. For most herbs and leafy greens, the seedling to harvest cycle can be as short as 21 days.

5). Grow sustainably and use up to 98% less water.
With closed-loop technology, the systems recycle water and nutrients. In turn, they use up to 98% less water than conventional farms, which is especially critical for those growing in drought-stricken regions.

6). Choose from more than 150 plants.
Many hydroponic farming systems limit what you can grow. But Abundance Farms supports more than 150 different plants — from delicate herbs and greens to hearty fruiting crops, such as tomatoes and squash. As a result, you can adapt your crop selection strategy on the fly to meet market demand.

7 Cultivate a superior product that sells at a premium price. When you grow an urban farm, you reduce food transportation time. That means your produce retains peak freshness and flavor. Plus, aeroponic methods actually increase the nutrient density of some crops, such as kale, tomatoes, and squash.

8). Invest in a farm that lasts a lifetime.
Unlike most white plastics used in agriculture — which degrade with time and

solar radiation — the FDA food grade-compliant, UV-stabilized plastic we use is designed to survive decades, so you can focus on farming, not replacing equipment every season.

9). Prevent common farming problems.
By growing crops off the ground, you reduce the risk of soil-borne pests and plant diseases. And since each tower grows independently, you can isolate and address any issues that do arise without jeopardizing your entire farm (unlike many hydroponic systems, which connect growing units to a common reservoir — allowing problems to spread and wipe out a farm overnight).

10). Start small and scale up.
The Abundance Farms turnkey vertical aeroponic farm comes with everything you need to get growing. And since the system is modular, you can start small with only a few towers, safely test the market and perfect your approach, and then scale up your farm (and success) when you feel ready.

11). Control the growing climate and ensure reliable results.
For soil-based farmers, a change in weather can be the difference between a record harvest and a debilitating season. But with Abundance Farms, you never have to worry about droughts or floods. And if you grow indoors or in a greenhouse, you can even control temperature, light, humidity, and other variables to consistently produce predictable yields, regardless of the weather.

12). Simplify the farming process.
Farming is hard work. But Abundance Farms makes it easier by automating feeding and watering cycles, eliminating weeding and digging, and minimizing pest risk. And if you need help along the way, you'll have full access to our farming resources and guidance from fellow farmerpreneurs.

WHAT CAN I GROW?

Fruits and Vegetables
Amaranth (vegetable type), Arugula, Beans: Lima, bush, pole, shell, fava, green, Broccoli, Broccoli Raab, Brussels Sprouts, Cabbage and Chinese cabbage, Cauliflower, Chard,- all types, Chicory, Collards, Cucumbers, Cress, Dandelion - Italian, Eggplant, European and Asian, Endive, Escarole, Garbanzo beans, Gourds, edible and ornamental, Kale, Kinh gioi, Kohlrabi, Komatsuna, Leeks, Lettuce - all types, Mesclun Varieties, Melons - all types, Misome, Mizuna, Mustard Greens, Okra, Pak Choi, Peas - all types, Peppers - all types, Radicchio, Sorrel, Spinach, Squash - all types, Strawberries, Tomatoes - all types

Herbs
Angelica, Anise Hyssop, Basil - all types, Bee Balm, Borage, Calendula, Catmint, Catnip, Chamomile, Chervil, Chives, Cilantro (Coriander) and Culantro, Citrus Basil, Cumin, Cutting Celery, Dandelion, Dill, Echinacea

(Coneflower), Epazote, Feverfew, Flax, Garlic Chives, Goldenseal, Hyssop, Lavender, Leaf Fennel, Lemon Balm, Lemon Grass, Lovage, Marjoram, Mexican Mint Marigold, Mibura, Milk Thistle, Mint - all varieties, Nettle, Oregano, Parsley (leafy types only), Passion Flower, Pleurisy Root, Pyrethrum, Rosemary, Rue, Sage, Salad Burnet, Saltwort, Savory, Shiso, Stevia, Thyme, Valerian, Wormwood

Flowers
Ageratum, Agrostemma, Ammi, Amaranth, Amaranthus, Artemisia, Aster, Bells of Ireland ,Bupleurum, Calendula, Carthamus, Cardoon, Centaurea, Celosia ,Coleus, Cosmos ,Craspedia, Datura, Delphinium, Eucalyptus, Euphorbia, Forget-me-not, Hibiscus, Impatiens, Kale - ornamental, Mondarda, Morning Glory, Nasturtiums, Nigella, Pansies, Petunia ,Phlox, Poppy, Polygonum, Ptilotus, Safflower, Salpiglossis, Rudbeckia, Salvia, Scabiosa, Scarlet Runner Bean, Snapdragon, Statice, Stock, Strawflower, Sunflowers (dwarf varieties only), Sweet Peas, Thunbergia, Verbena, Viola, Yarrow, Zinnia

The Favor Path
Mere months before the company that developed and manufactures the vertical aeroponic towers decided to expand their market from residential scale to community and commercial scale I discovered them and built relationships with top management. At the same time I was introduced to key national and international contacts that were looking for a safer and more productive technology for growing food.

Covenant Relationships
As mentioned before often FAVOR acts as a magnet to attract people who are on the same frequency resulting in Covenant Relationships. This certainly proved to be true for Abundance Farms. Although the frequency attraction often meant that a friendship was formed within 10 minutes of first meeting, the Covenant Relationship building did take time to mature.

The collection of initial Covenant Relationships was not the typical or usual business plan targeted referrals. It was not agricultural expertise or business management advisors or venture capital investors. More importantly the frequency magnet was actually based on the power of agreement of married business couples. The married couple of Gary & Sue were in agreement on the value terms of the Abundance Economy and that frequency attracted likeminded Abundance couples in university education and vocational training, retreat centers for mind and body and soul, affordable housing projects, community food banks, abundance-based financial systems. This handful of Covenant Relationship couples have already led to the opportunity to develop dozens of Abundance-based farms. The second level of introductions from these couples is now leading to national and international contacts that lay the foundation for hundreds and thousands of Abundance-based farms in the coming years of Abundance.

Alignment of Assignments

As the Covenant Relationships matured it was discovered that there were synergistic and complimentary visions of what the couples were pursuing. We were not looking for each other but we found that our assignments and our spheres of influence were aligned with the other couple assignments and spheres of influence. Education and training programs were looking for new appropriate technologies like aeroponic vertical food production, to prepare their students for careers; remote retreat centers were looking for sustainable food sources that also offer therapeutic value; affordable housing projects were looking for food security answers for individual homeowners, neighborhood groupings and community food banks; new financial and treasury systems were looking for technologies that are sustainable and contribute to community needs while offering shared equity or profit sharing for all who contribute.

Agreement and Collaboration

A perfect example of how FAVOR leads to Covenant Relationships which leads to Alignment of Assignments which leads to Agreement and Collaboration is the following. In August 2018 I was in a conference in Calgary, Canada when I met an evangelist from Denver, Colorado. As we were sharing what we were doing I shared my thoughts about Abundance and what I was planning for Abundance Farms in Spring 2019.

This marketplace minister was from India and wished to explore Abundance Farms for India. A pastor's wife from South Africa was following the Denver evangelist on Facebook and invited him to preach at their church. He did and became friends with the pastor and his wife.

For about seven years the South African pastor had held on to a vision of a training center which included greenhouses. Also, before meeting with the Denver evangelist, the pastor had been summoned to a meeting with the King of the largest kingdom in South Africa. The King asked the pastor if he could find people who could invest in businesses that could be located in his kingdom for his people.

The Denver evangelist gave the pastor and his wife our information for Abundance Farms. He was prompted to contact me in late 2018 and we met in the Mesa, AZ at our Tower Farms training center. As a result, the pastor and his wife signed a Memorandum of Agreement & Collaboration (MOA&C) which led to the formation of Abundance Farms South Africa and the Abundance Holding Company. This has resulted in the identification and vetting of nearly 50 candidates for Abundance Farms in South Africa and surrounding countries.

Abundance Economy Model

This MOA&C represents one of five foundational couple-based Covenant Relationships for replication for several hundred community and commercial

Abundance Farms. Abundance Farms LLC shares a 20% ownership with 80% ownership for local Collaborators. One of the primary guidelines is not to let your growth out pace your Agreement & Collaboration. All the foundational flagship Abundance Farms are organized and operated on the primary values of Agreement, no debt or loan instruments, shared responsibility and shared rewards of success including 30% Pay It Forward investments into the community and into replication of sustainable complimentary collaborations who will in turn Pay It Forward.

Successful Abundance Farms may also take the form of sustainable food banks, Community Hybrid Corporation farms where a percentage of sales are for profit which supports a percentage of not-for-profit food distribution, neighborhood and community member-based food farms, corporate and institutional farms for employees and families, and profit-sharing commercial farms.

Reborne Global Trust Evergreen Fund
Founded by Dr. Gary and Sue Sorensen 2020

Reborne Global Trust's vision is to develop an evergreen (self-sustaining) fund based on secured and donated assets to finance "seed money for equity" that results in the commercialization and deployment of sustainable and "disruptive" technologies and projects and corporations that will be viable global economic, humanitarian, social and environmental stewardship models that in replication may serve with positive effects for employment and improved quality of life in developed and emerging countries.

The Reborne Global Trust Evergreen Fund (RGT-EF) www.reborne.us has a philosophy similar to the Unified Investment Strategy (UIS) recently adopted by the Center for Social Innovation, Graduate School of Business, Stanford University. This Creative Equilibrium model developed for organizations such as Reborne Global Trust focuses on creating financial, social, environmental and humanitarian values for measuring the success of a venture.

The 4 areas of focus for the RGT-Evergreen Fund are currently the following:

1). Global Solutions for Energy

   Over 1.2 billion people are without access to electricity worldwide, most of them concentrated in about a dozen countries in Africa and Asia. Another 2.8 billion rely on wood or other biomass for cooking and heating, resulting in indoor and outdoor air pollution attributable for 4.3 million deaths a year.The World Bank Group supports the Sustainable Energy for All initiative, and is committed to work towards accomplishing the initiative's three goals by 2030:

   1. universal access to electricity and clean cooking fuels,
   2. doubling the share of the world's energy supplied by renewable sources from 18% to 36%, and
   3. doubling the rate of improvement in energy efficiency.

   Eighty-five countries have opted-in to this initiative, and many public, private and non-governmental actors are supporting its implementation. Energy generation, transmission, storage and utilization of all forms of energy is now one of the major economic powers of all countries around the globe. Disruptive technologies are constantly fighting for their position in the marketplace. The risks are great but so are the potential rewards. One of the primary tasks of the RGT-Evergreen Fund is to search, identify, review and evaluate the disruptive, cutting edge energy technologies that could have global impact. The embryonic stage funding will select technologies that have passed the proof of concept and bench scale tests and are ready to move on to commercial prototype production. The established stage funding will select proven commercial prototypes that are ready for mass commercial production.

2. Global Solutions for Water (mswg.reborne.us)

   Access to safe water is measured by the number of people who have a reasonable means of getting an adequate amount of water that is safe for drinking, washing, and essential household activities, expressed as a percentage of the total population. It reflects the health of a country's people and the country's capacity to collect, clean, and distribute water to consumers.

   Water is essential for life, yet more than 1.4 billion people in low- and middle-income countries and an additional 50 million people in high-income countries lack access to safe water for drinking, personal hygiene and domestic use. In addition, close to 2 billion people do not have access to adequate sanitation facilities.

   Safe water includes treated surface water, as well as untreated but uncontaminated water from sources such as natural springs and sanitary wells. On average, a person needs about 20 liters of safe water each day to meet his or her metabolic, hygienic, and domestic needs. Without safe water, people cannot lead healthy, productive lives. For example, an estimated 900 million people suffer and approximately 2 million die from water-related diarrheal illnesses each year. Most, but not all, of these people live in low- and middle-income countries, and those at greatest risk are children and the elderly. Millions more people worldwide suffer from other water-related diseases, such as bilharzia, cholera, elephantiasis, and hookworm.

Moreover, the rapid growth of cities throughout the world can strain the capacity of governments to provide adequate sanitary facilities, leaving inhabitants, especially the poor, to live amid unhealthy open sewage ditches. Untreated sewage also tends to contaminate the water reserves closest to the cities, forcing communities to pipe water from further and further away as cities expand. The competition for water use from residential, institutional, commercial, industrial, agricultural and recreational and ecosystem demands is placing a premium value on ingenuity and resourcefulness in being a good steward of water. Desalination, membrane distillation, reuse, recycling and resource recovery technologies are prime candidates for selection for RGT-EF.

3). Global Solutions for Life
Wellness Technologies for Food Production and Nutrition
Add global nutrition and food access to the RGT-EF area of focus to fight the epidemic of worldwide malnutrition. Today, twenty-five million children around the globe are malnourished due to food access issues. Malnutrition negatively effects proper physical and cognitive development. This leaves those with lesser access to education at an even higher vulnerability.

Cognitive and physical development are essential for future success. Estimates are that more than 50 million children under the age of five suffer from chronic malnutrition. Each year, 3.5 million children die of malnutrition related causes.

Ironically however, obesity and under-nutrition affect billions of people and threaten a global health catastrophe. With the world's population expected to reach nine billion by 2050 and food production stagnating, global food production will have to increase by an estimated 70 per cent to keep pace with increasing demand. As well, the food system will need to change dramatically to effectively deliver safer, more nutritious food to consumers.

Nearly one billion people, one out of six globally, lack access to adequate food and nutrition. By 2050, the global population will surpass nine billion people, and demand for agricultural products is expected to double.

In addition to increasing overall production, there is a growing focus on increasing the nutritional value of food produced and on understanding changing consumer food preferences as countries become more affluent.

Technology alone is not the answer, but can contribute to the solution. New disruptive technologies for food production, processing, storage, access and delivery and nutrition bio-availability may well be critical for meeting the human population needs in decades to come.

4). Global Solutions for Living

By 2030, 3 billion people, about 40% of the world's population, will need new housing and basic urban infrastructure and services. Breaking down the numbers translates to a current annual need for 14 million new houses and a conservative estimate of $420 billion in total investment needed. The urgency and magnitude of the need for affordable housing in the coming decades is clear.

The Housing Sector is a significant contributor to economic growth and has multiplier effects on the broader economy. Studies suggest that in the U.S., every dollar spent on housing generates as much as $1.60 in the wider economy.

Housing development creates jobs and supports economic inclusion. From direct to indirect jobs and skilled to unskilled jobs, the impact of housing on job creation is clear. In India, it is estimated that the impact of 2 million new affordable homes would be direct employment for 3 million people working in construction, indirect employment for 24 million people in linked industries and services (wood, steel, paint, electricity etc.), and a 2% growth in gross domestic product (GDP).

Despite these obvious benefits, there are still global constraints in building more affordable housing, both on the demand and supply side. Demand constraints are usually related to finance. Housing finance has very low penetration in emerging economies, typically less than 5% of the adult population has a loan to purchase housing, compared to 25-35% in U.S., Canada, and Western Europe. On the supply side, there are constraints related to land and property rights limiting the development of large-scale affordable developments, and regulatory obstacles that present difficulties in registering land titles and/or outdated building codes and planning regulations.

However, there are technology breakthroughs for housing that both reduce the cost of housing while using more locally available materials, reducing energy consumption and providing healthier living environment.

Providing housing for 3 Billion people by 2030 is both a challenge and an opportunity. It is not an impossible feat, but one that can be overcome, to develop technology systems that increase access to sustainable housing in the developing world, and affordable housing opportunities for all.

EVERGREEN FUNDING

Reborne Global Trust Evergreen Fund is not an Angel Investment Fund. It does not consider solicited proposals. The RGT Wisdom & Knowledge Council monitors the technologies in the four areas of focus by a combination of sophisticated data mining services and a network of legacy advisors. RGTEF may match identified technologies with compatible existing companies, combine several breakthrough technologies into viable licensed projects, or even be the catalyst for launching embryonic businesses.

The "seed money" for funding will not demand loan interest payments from the RGT-EF funded projects or companies but the principal must be scheduled to Pay It Forward as well as assigning a reasonable agreed percentage of equity and licensing rights to RGT-EF in order to continue the legacy growth and impact of the RGT-Evergreen Fund.

The Favor Path

Although Reborne Global Trust was formed in 2008 the RGT Evergreen Fund was created in 2020 as by-product of my research into Abundance. Initially discussion with some members of the RGT Wisdom & Knowledge Council cast the ideas for "Seed Money for Equity". Mixed in were discussions with some pioneers in marketplace Kingdom businesses.

Covenant Relationships

The steering groups that helped give definition to the RGT Evergreen Fund concept was the Covenant Relationship KDLA (Dr. Karl Bandlien, Dr. Stan Jeffery, John Anderson and myself) and New Kingdom Global (Dr. Stan Jeffery and international membership), and some individual members from Kingdom Congressional International Alliance.

Alignment of Assignments

RGT and NKG had several levels of Alignment of Assignments resulting in RGT Evergreen Fund narrowing its focus while combing NKG to form the Abundance Research Institute. RGT Evergreen Fund would select individuals with embryonic and early-stage technologies within its 4 Areas of Focus. NKG would mentor individuals through the commercialization process and John Anderson and GDP would assist in launching sustainable businesses for the technologies.

Agreement and Collaboration

Although RGT Evergreen Fund is still pursuing its own internal funding and donation sources, it is also working with NKG and GDP funding sources including Legacy Benefactor Collaborators. Eventually the "Seed Money for Equity" returns will become the major source of perpetuating funds.

Abundance Economy Model: As stated previously the RGT Evergreen Fund is the prototype for a perpetual not for profit "Seed Money for Equity" Community Hybrid Statutory Trust.

Living Space Initiative (LSI) and LSI for Adaptive Reuse
Founded by Dr. Gary Sorensen and Howard Selman 2008, 2020

The Living Space Initiative (LSI) 2008

PROJECT DESCRIPTION:

The Living Space Initiative (LSI) project envisions transforming "empty big box buildings" into living spaces tailored for specific community needs. Rather than just a housing project, LSI adopts the philosophy of the Unified Investment Strategy (UIS) recently adopted by the Center for Social Innovation, Graduate School of Business, Stanford University. This model developed for foundations such as Reborne Global Trust focuses on creating financial, social, environmental and humanitarian values for measuring the success of a venture.

The LSI project permits us to think "outside" the box, and "inside" the box. The LSI project not only evaluates and considers the community needs in the design criteria, but it actually enlists the participation of community leaders and support organizations in the design, development, construction and ongoing use of each local project. Volunteerism can be an integral part of the housing, educational, medical, recreational, environmental and social needs of the stakeholders of the project.

In an effort to create "Zero Net Energy" projects, LSI's will use a collective of local projects to investment in alternative energy projects that would generate excess electricity to more than offset the local power usage of each box. Roof rainwater runoff will be captured for landscaping maintenance. Former parking lots will become community gardens, green spaces and playground areas for the community.

A mixed-use development of storefront businesses inside the LSI "mall" and outside on pad sites and adjacent properties will provide supporting medical, educational and consumer services not only for the LSI residents but also for the surrounding neighborhood and community.

The objective of this venture is to create a model which can be implemented and/or modified to address the utilization of tens of thousands of strip commercial and big box centers that are vacant, brownfields/greenfields, surplus federal property, closed military bases, underutilized campgrounds, warehouses, large utilitarian structures, rural and historic properties.

The project real estate trust (*Reborne Global Trust*, Delaware) has been established to aid the various tax-exempt corporations that are required to finance, own, operate and maintain the project(s), such as a community land trust (CLT) that is a private, nonprofit organization that buys land and holds it in trust for the benefit of a community. Community land trust developments come in a variety of shapes and sizes. They have been used in urban neighborhoods and in rural settings for housing projects. A CLT could be the perpetual owner of the LSI housing projects developed.

- Executive Summary of LSI Project

Living Space Initiative for Adaptive Reuse 2020
www.reborne.us/lsi

BENEFITS TO LOCAL AND NATIONAL ECONOMIES
The main value of these specific Living Space Initiative projects is to provide affordable housing for our veterans and their families and working families of modest means in a safe, secure and sustainable community. Besides the immediate jobs created for design, construction and management of the facilities, many of the projects will provide employment opportunities for service providers and retail entrepreneurs. In many communities the projects will remodel or readapt existing vacant buildings thus giving life to dead or dying areas of the community. The LSI will become the anchor to encourage compatible development in the surrounding area. The LSI developments will serve as templates to be replicated.

LEGACY RESOURCE PARTNERS
Reborne Global Trust Evergreen Fund is looking for corporate, private foundation and individual **Legacy Resource Partners** to successfully execute the development of the RGT EF portfolio in agreement and collaboration with the New Kingdom Group Treasury. Contributions may be in the form of donated corporate equity, licensing rights, property assets to be liquidated or used as a platform for projects, corporate team partnering for R&D and commercialization efforts, and direct financial support. There is no direct return on investments for the contributors to the RGT Evergreen Fund. However, the **Legacy Resource Partners** will be privy to the RGT-EF technologies, projects and companies for consideration for further future private investments.

The Favor Path
In late 2007 Howard Selman, a business friend of mine, and I began to talk about what he might want to do as he approached traditional retirement age. The discussion moved in the direction of Legacy impact and what that might mean for the time beyond our careers. At the time Howard was living near Bentonville, Arkansas where Walmart has its headquarters. The week we started discussing a concept of turning empty "big box" stores into revitalized

mixed use communities, Howard happened to meet the Director of Real Estate Properties for Walmart. Howard mentioned our concept to him, and he invited us to make a more formal presentation. What resulted is that Howard and I formed Reborne Global Trust and created the concept we named "The Living Space Initiative (LSI)", which we presented in early 2008. At the time Walmart had over 400 "dark stores" per year because they were growing into new Super Stores and vacating existing stores. The LSI was a perfect match for our Legacy intentions.

Covenant Relationships

The initial FAVOR introduction led to further introductions to the primary Walmart Architectural and Engineering firm, major national CPA firm, major national law firm, major national real estate firm and major national public relations firm. Just as we were about to launch our LSI Collaboration the "Economic Bubble of 2008 hit and dissipated our plans. However, it did not dissipate our relationships. The change also allowed us to expand our LSI concept to develop relationships with individuals interested in affordable housing for the homeless, veterans, seniors, working and special medical needs families. Besides national firms specializing in sustainable and eco-friendly designs we now have relationships with regional and targeted smaller local design firms that may be mentored by the larger firms. As the Abundance Economy approaches, we have now attracted relationships with Legacy Investment Collaborators.

Alignment of Assignments

We now have a Gathering of Solutions awaiting the Collaboration that comes from Abundance. The Collaborations will bring an acceleration of successful replications.

Agreement and Collaboration

The key to LSI developments is an Agreement with Collaborations among the private, public and government sectors. We will not move forward with projects that have resistance or conflict or cannot come into Agreement to operate with Abundance values.

Abundance Economy Model

As scale and circumstances may vary the LSI may be structured under a private Pay It Forward Model that manages the Collaboration with public and governmental agencies. This may be converted to management by a Community Hybrid Corporation as long as the dispersion of profit funds follow the All Shall Prosper for ownership, workers, community and designated Pay It Forward sustainable entities, whether LSI replication or complimentary entities.

ThermoNeutronics LLC
Founded by Dr. Gary Sorensen, Howard Selman and Randy Horsak 2013

THERMONEUTRONICS

www.reborne.us/tn

INTRODUCTION
Advances in science and engineering have changed our world.

For example, rudimentary propeller airplanes gave way to high performance propeller aircraft which gave way to jet engine aircraft, missiles, rockets, and lunar landing modules.

In perhaps an even greater way, nano technology will change the world. It is changing the world as you read this document, but it will materially change the world in the future.

ThermoNeutronics will become part of that change mechanism, by introducing radically different nano technology into rapidly changing solar energy and related markets, by offering Generation III solar and associated technology.

Generation I is the conventional silicon-based solar cells that have evolved over the past decades, and are widely deployed. Generation II is the advent of the use of film, nano, and other technologies in an attempt to overcome inherent limitations of Generation I technology.

ThermoNeutronics' technologies are best termed "next generation, Generation III."

Our developmental technologies have been patented by Dr. Somenath Mitra and others, and include:

- Carbon nanotube organic photovoltaic technology (CNT-OPV)
- Carbon nanotube infrared light based organic photovoltaic technology (CNT-IR OPV)
- Carbon nanotube glare / shading control technology (CNT-GSC)
- Carbon nanotube thermal circuitry (CNT-TC)
- Carbon nanotube alkaline battery technology (CNT-AB)

- Carbon nanotube lithium rechargeable battery technology (CNT-LRB)
- Carbon nanotube membrane desalination technology (CNT-MD)
- Proprietary integration of these emerging technologies
- Morphilm®
- Innovative motor design (CNT-IMD)
- Thermal circuitry and thermo-neutronic applications (TC / TN)

WHAT IS THE TECHNOLOGY?

Carbon nanotubes are unique, one-dimensional systems of pure carbon (graphene) with technology disruptive optical, mechanical, and electrical properties. To grasp this technology, think in terms of "how small is small" — specifically, things that are several nanometers in size. A single nanometer is equivalent to 0.00000003937 (3.937 10e-8) inches. Conversely, one inch is 25,400,000 nanometers.

Some typical nanotube configurations are shown below.

Carbon graphene can be rolled into "tube-like" configurations that have diameters on the order of 1 to 100 nm and lengths of 1 nm to almost 20 centimeters in length (about 8 inches). They can be arranged on this micro-scale in all sorts of configurations, ranging from the simple to extremely complex. They can be integrated with other chemical substances to enhance their properties.

Carbon nanotubes are the strongest and stiffest materials discovered to date in terms of tensile strength and elasticity. They have more than 1000 times the conductivity of copper or aluminum wire. They can be configured to absorb or block electromagnetic radiation, such as radar. They can be configured as good thermal insulators, or as good thermal conductors. They can be used to fabricate solar cells, and batteries, and to treat water.

So what can you do with all of this?

The bottom line — scientists and engineers are using this micro-sized technology to do things that conventional, visible technology cannot do. For example, in 2011, scientists and engineers built the world's smallest rotational electric motor. The motor was about 1 nm in diameter.

MARKETS FOR THERMONEUTRONICS" TECHNOLOGY

There is a flurry of research and development, commercialization, and investment in nano technology. With leap-frogging technology, the world is rapidly changing from
conventional technologies to new emerging technologies that create vast new markets and materially change the world in which we live.

The primary markets for technologies envisioned by ThermoNeutronics are enormous. This is critical in assessing the viability of our technologies since the development of high-tech solutions for limited applications may not necessarily make sense, except possibly for "boutique" applications, such as space exploration and medicine.

Energy Sector
On the other hand, huge markets exist that can accommodate new CNT-based technologies. For example, the application of solar power systems has greatly increased over the past decade, but the cost of solar energy is still expensive, relative to conventional base-load fossil fueled power plants. However, with Generation III technology, that could well change, with CNT technology providing more economical power systems that could be even more economical than conventional power generation.

ThermoNeutronics' CNT-OPV, CNT-IR-OPV, CNT-AB, and CNT-RLB patented technologies offer huge opportunities in the energy sector by providing Generation III solar and battery technologies. These systems provide for higher overall electrical yields and efficiencies, which, in turn, lead to lower overall installation and energy production costs. Imagine solar systems that capture sunlight energy during cloudy or nighttime conditions.

And, imagine solar cell and battery systems that are the size of a postage stamp, and that can be printed in the field using a conventional ink jet printer.

Residential and Commercial Buildings Sector
When integrated with other technologies such as thermo-neutronics and heat circuitry, the application of CNT-based solar and battery technologies offer enormous opportunities in both residential and commercial building construction. Decades ago, single-pane glass windows were the norm. Today, multi-pane windows and solar window films have widespread application throughout the world due to their energy saving properties. CNTbased technology will only expand and enhance those applications.

ThermoNeutronics' CNT-GSC, thermal circuitry, and thermo-neutronics technologies offer opportunities in building construction by providing the next generation technology.

Imagine window films that not only block the sun, but capture energy from the sun to generate electricity for the building, and store that energy for nighttime use, and also have the ability to utilize shading control for optimum use of sunlight conditions throughout the year, and throughout the day.

Water Purification and Desalination Sector
Along with energy, the availability of pure drinking water is the greatest challenge in the world. CNT-based technologies offer significant advantages over conventional
technologies such as reverse osmosis in terms of smaller size, lower capital cost, reduced fouling, lower electricity requirements, and superior economics.

As such, this technology may lead to economical desalination of brackish and seawater, providing much needed water for agriculture and human consumption.

ThermoNeutronics' CNT-MD offers exciting cutting-edge technology that can be developed and scaled for small residential and large commercial desalination systems. The technology also has tremendous application in industry, for example, the treatment of frack water and produced water in oil and gas environments. Imagine the impact of CNT-based technology in the water treatment sector, that would provide additional water resources as a result of more effective and efficient technology.

Innovative Electric Motor Design

ThermoNeutronics has teamed with the inventor of a high efficiency electrical motor. CNT conductors can be incorporated into the motor windings. Imagine a motor the size of a coffee cup with the same horsepower as a conventional motor the size of a gallon milk jug. The potential market is enormous, ranging from hair dryers to washing machines to large industrial motors.

The Favor Path

Although I had been working with some of the concepts for ThermoNeutronics for several years, it was in 2012-2013 that I receive 2 major FAVOR introductions. A friend sent me an email video of an NJIT Professor, Dr. Somenath Mitra, who was using carbon nanotubes (CNT) to create paintable solar shingles. I made contact with him and upon and initial in person visit we realized that CNT-based ThermoNeutronics were very viable. During that same year I was arranging meetings between my friend Joseph Fournier and members of the Nuclear Engineering Department at Texas A&M University where I taught for almost 20 years. The discussion was about Joseph's Modular Pebble Bed Reactor, but one of the young professors, Dr. Pavel Tsvetkov, was also an expert in calculating heat flow characteristics in boilers and nuclear reactors. On a follow up visit, we discovered that he could be instrumental in developing theoretical and mathematical models of the ThermoNeutronic concepts.

Covenant Relationships and Alignment of Assignment

As the relationship developed with Dr. Mitra I found that his research also crossed over into ThermoNeutronic CNT-based membranes for water desalination and treatment trains for treating contaminated waters. Dr. Tsvetkov have maintained contact to propose joint TAMU and ThermoNeutronics research for using ThermoNeutronic concept in designing nuclear reactors and for hiding heat signatures for stealth vehicles and combat vests for the Department of Defense. In addition, a covenant relationship with Mike Kramer that was initiated from a common interest in fly ash technology has 20 years later resulted in the possible use of ThermoNeutronic-based wiring being integrated into his Delta Force (Attractive Magnet) Motors.

Agreement and Collaboration
ThermoNeutronics LLC currently has Agreements to Collaborate with Dr. Som Mitra, Dr. Pavel Tsvetkov and Mike Kramer.

Abundance Economy Model
ThermoNeutronics LLC is using the Pay It Forward Model using a profit dispersion model of 30:10:30:30 with 30% being invested forward into sustainable Pay It Forward businesses. The IP developed is also shared with participating, contributing and supporting University and Research agencies.

Likewise, the IP seeds are planted in our Collaborators that they may grow fruit of new innovations and technologies beyond the scope of ThermoNeutronics LLC.

Abundance Research Institute 2020
Founded by Dr. Stan Jeffery, CEO, New Kingdom Global
Dr. Gary Sorensen, CEO, Reborne Global Trust

FOUNDATIONAL CONCEPT

To facilitate the research into visionary technologies in areas that will give glory to God. These could include health, food production, environmental, housing areas that benefit people and the "natural" God created environment

Anything that does not benefit the world will not be considered. These includes weapons, practices that are not environmentally sustainable, drugs that do not promote health and well-being and anything counter to the word of God.

In addition to promoting research and providing funding, guidance and facilities the institute seeks to help researchers develop products and practices into sustainable business.

At all stages of development researchers will be encouraged to consider how to develop a business that can be developed from their research that will provide income and employment.

They will also be encouraged to mentor others who may benefit from their experience and insights.

If the researcher does not wish to follow through and take the results of their research to the business development stage, they will be encouraged to allow others to do so. To this end assistance will be given to find suitable business partners and negotiate suitable agreements

Thus, the two basic concepts of the Research Institute are the proving of ideas through direct and methodical research and the development of subsequent businesses that can create income and employment.

At all times the practices and procedures must be ethical and sustainable and benefit the world. To this end best practices of the Kingdom of God and the world will be promoted and combined where appropriate.

LOCATION

The vision for the Research Institute is that it will have global reach. Research is happening and visions are found in many places. Those with specific needs are often those who come up with the ideas to meet the needs. To this end it is not possible to limit the researchers to one location.

The researcher may know the best facilities support and structure and needs that can be fulfilled close to home.

- Field trial will be best conducted where the conditions are optimum - these are usually found in the researchers' home location.
- Experts who can verify the technical aspects of the research may best be found in the researcher's home location.
- Material and equipment to conduct the research may best be found in the local environment.
- Support structures and networks of technical personnel may best be found close to home.
- Experts in business practices and conditions need to have local knowledge and accreditation.

Unless the researcher needs or wants to move to a new location, support may best be found in their own environment. The Institute central administration will help with the establishment of facilities, research guidelines, the establishment of KPI, finding mentors, establishment of business goals and documentation.

There will also be need to established regular reporting and oversight practice. These will need to be administered from a central environment.

A central management / administrative facility will be established in Sydney, Australia. This will include the managerial and administration offices and support staff. It will include facilities for meetings, training programs and research facilities for those who wish to be located in Sydney.

Assistance will be given to those who wish to relocate to Sydney. However, those who wish to come from other countries must meet the immigration requirements of the Australian Government. This must be done through their own endeavors, however, some advice and guidance will be offered. There is not a guarantee of financial assistance, although this may be offered at the discretion of the Institute.

CANDIDATE PERSONNEL

As part of the application process each proposal for research funding and entry into the Research Institute community must include a description of personnel requirements. This should include a statement regarding their role, qualifications, responsibilities, time requirements and the facilities required. These should be reasonable and in line with the notion that the operation is small and at a start-up stage. It is not a case of many hands make light work. But all involved must be willing to participate in the ancillary tasks of running the operation. The "Head researcher" may have to be the "chief bottle washer".

If the business is located in an incubator style of facility, reception and answering services may be available on a shared basis.

Where possible those who can provide legal and accounting services will be recommended to the applicant. Advice on fees will be included in the recommendation.

Applicants will always be required to establish a professional operation that will stand up to the requirements of a legal operation in their area. These need to be established at the start and not left to be sorted out at a later stage. Remember those who offer their services for free usually reasonably expect some recognition when the profits start to flow. All expectations should be clearly established at the beginning.

In addition, legal requirements should be clearly established. The aim of the training programs offered by the Institute are to help in the establishment of a sustainable business. Ensuring that the above mentioned legal and relationships issues are an essential part of this as they can affect the reputation and legal status of the business in the future.

Participation in the Training programs are an essential KPI for any business that is part of the Institute funding program.

FUNDING

The Institute will be funded by a privately established fund designed to cover the ongoing costs of running the Institute and the cost of research.

All financial matters will be fully compliant with the country of residence (the Institute). Researchers will be expected to ensure that their personal and business finances are fully compliant with their country of residence.

Researchers will also be expected to fulfil any conditions associated with their funding that the Institute applies. Any funding offers to researcher is for the purpose of specific research and is not to provide the researcher with a "lifestyle". One of the KPI for future funding will be detailed financial accounts. (details will be provided).

However, in some circumstances living expenses may form a component of the research funding.

Funding will be released to the researcher in stages with well-defined goals for each tranche of funding. The KPIs will be clearly articulated and reporting requirement clearly defined. They will include written reports, financial reports, demonstrations, face to face meetings, interviews etc.

As each of the goals is reached the requirement for the next stage of funding will be provided.

Should the researcher have difficulty reaching their next stage of research in the time frame specified it is expected that a report will be made in a timely manner. With the reasons for the delay explained, as there can be many reasons for the delays, it may be possible to negotiate another date for the next refinancing phase.

EDUCATION AND TRAINING PROGRAM

Having a good idea does not necessarily mean the potential researcher will know how to go about doing the research and developing the idea into a successful business.

To this end one of the conditions under which funding is offered is that the researchers undergo training programs. These will be specified and offered by the Research Institute. The cost of these programs will be covered by the research funding.
These funds will be specified in the funding details but will in fact not be paid directly to the researcher. This cannot be used for any other purpose.

Participation in development programs will form part of the KPIs for the next stage of funding.

One of the cornerstones of the Research Institute is that the research leads to the development of sustainable business. To this end it is important that the end result of the research is compliant with government and industry requirements.

In addition to business issues which must be clear and legal, there must be clear ownership of the IP. Company ownership, payment expectations from any previous funders must be clear, roles and responsibilities must be clearly articulated.

It must be clear and documented what each participant has contributed and what they expect in return.

The Research Institute will specify and offer the program that it requires participant to undertake, there will be no exceptions.

ORGANIZATIONAL STRUCTURE

The Research Institute will consist of a small management team to conduct the day-to-day operations of the Institute. The detailed makeup of the Institute staff will be developed when a location is found, the accommodation that can be offered is finalized and the number of researchers who wish to be located in Sydney is known.

The role of the Institute staff will be one of oversight communications and a level of support.

Other services will be provided by a recommended provider:
- Legal
- Accounting
- Development programs

Compliance issues the researchers will need to source individual or bodies who can provide compliance certification. However, the Institute will endeavor to assist the process.

Researchers who are located overseas will need to find local providers of services. However, the Institute will provide assistance where it can.

The Research Institute is in the development concept stage. It is envisaged that as needs are identified the personnel and services provided will develop to meet the needs of participants as the budget allows.

OVERSIGHT

The purpose of the oversight in both research and business development area is to help ensure the success of each project.

To this end, it is important that the best practitioners available are used. The Institute will recommend suitable advisors such as legal accounting mentors etc. However, should a researcher wish to use other service providers the Institute reserves the right to assess the suitability of the provider. The provider must understand and be willing to abide by the ethos of the Institute. In addition, they must be suitably accredited in their area of expertise.

Where technical and research oversight is required those offering, oversight must be suitable qualified in the areas. In addition to being supportive of the ethos and methods of the institute.

Types of Research

Three areas
1). Directed
These are based upon ideas that have merit and could be developed by a specialised research group

2). Assisted
These are possibly entrepreneurs who need assistance and support

3). Facilitated
These are companies who want to align with the NKGRI and benefit from the network and services

The Favor Path
The path to the kingdom abundance research institute was long and with many diversions. This has taken over 10 years of planning and growing the resource funding base in accordance with God's directions and favour.

This was via three world class technology parks the Australian Technology Park in Sydney, OptixLab in Malaysia and the University of Ballarat Technology Park in Victoria Australia. Each one of these has been a steep learning curve for a system that did not have any training courses (or anyone to follow) at the time. Only the guidance of our creator. The Eventual model shown is a distillation and combination of a number of incubators and technology park structures.

In essence it follows the growth of an idea through a research group to an incubator / start up facilitation centre to integrate with funding and then accelerating into the marketplace.

Selection
The typical selection process for projects includes intercessory input at some point in the process. See example below.

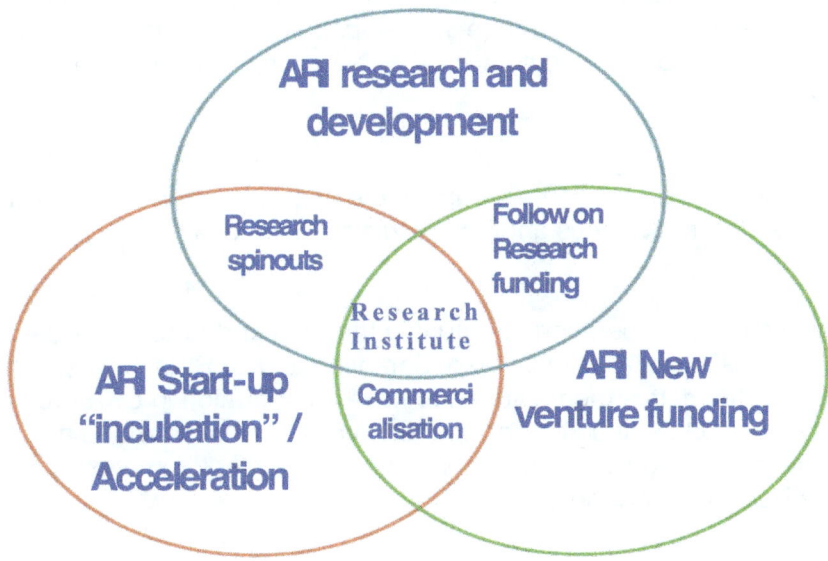

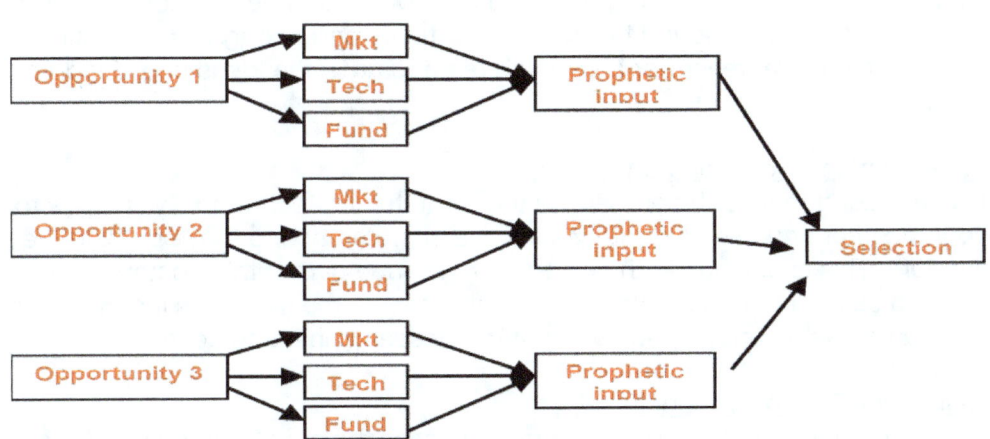

The example shows this after the due diligence but in many cases, this could also be before significant expenditure on analysis has been undertaken.
This is all predicated on the clear understanding that we ALL are focused on what our creator God requires is to grow and develop.

Covenant Relationships
The early connection with Dr Gary was via the KDLA Energy Tower assignment in Haifa Israel that grew out of the KCIA Science and Technology Group. It was

clear that we had a synergy and co-related experiences in the university and business world.

Each company that we fund/ resource will have a covenant agreement that enable us the share and develop relationships under the authority of the courts of heaven jurisdiction. This is shown in the New Kingdom Global part of this document.

Alignment of Assignments
There are two levels of alignments one is the operational structure and the second is ALL the investees and downstream operations.

One
The grouping of the operation structure in the USA and Australia is based around the desire and skill of Dr Gary Sorensen and Dr Stan Jeffery as the foundational team. It is then planned to have an operation in UK/Europe. The linking with GDP and HCN on the KDLA assignment provided a requirement and a source of new ideas and product requirements that will help drive the Research and the institution

Two
The alignment of the investee has been assessed and developed via the New Kingdom Global international round table monthly meetings. Here we can see those who have heart for others and the love of God being released. We are clearly looking for sound business opportunity and strong business skills either via the entrepreneur or a selected team to grow the ideas into kingdom businesses.

Agreement and Collaboration
It is envisaged that each company in the Institute and technopole will agree to work together and use each other's service in preference to those outside the kingdom. This is outlined in the kingdom exchange part of this document. The ability to us the token for collaboration with other in the system is incorporated in the agreements and expectations of the Research institute centres.

Abundance Economy Model
The model being developed to help other access the growth of the supported companies is linked to the current thoughts of equity-based DLT tokens/coins that have an asset based upon equity in start-up companies.

The basic idea in the abundance model is equity-based kingdom growth where all prosper. The idea of good seed and good ground with God provision can have 30-60-100 fold growth that is shared by all involved.

The plan is to help people move from a debt based central bank controlled system to a new equity based system working with the Kingdom Treasury.

New Kingdom Global Treasury
Founded by Dr. Stan Jeffery and Dr. Gary Sorensen 2018

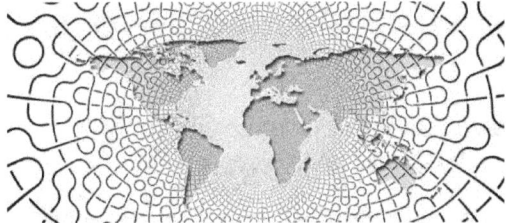

OBJECTIVE

To establish a world-wide financial structure (ARK) that will enable God's people to trade and store their treasure and participate in sound business opportunities backed by a token (gold / asset) based system. Let us pool our resources and energy as the "Body of Believers".

This is expected to integrate the many initiatives throughout the world that God has started.

They will form a NKG system of treasury and Research Institute and land / resources with oversight and ownership. The token needs to be translatable into physical exchangeable form if the current world financial system is unavailable to God's people.

BACKGROUND

There is sufficient evidence that the current system is not according to our creator's plan and is being made more corrupted each day. This has resulted in the people in many of God's Kingdom being disadvantaged in transactions and funding requirements. The basis of scripture Rev 13: 17 which we believe gives insight into the phase where we will not be able to trade with the existing world structure.
REQUIREMENT

Establish a for profit New Kingdom Treasury/Exchequer/Storehouse with returns based upon equity growth and equitable distribution of funding with low dependency on fiat currency or government support. This is not simply for profit, but for sound Kingdom growth.

The returns would be based upon operational profit from dividend returns and asset valuation growth and not a fixed interest.

Based upon the proposed financial plan the opportunity for initial investor/covenanters to add value either direct funding required or use services and/or current systems in exchange for equity participation. The founders may also be initial officers and therefore receive advisory and executive funding from the initial treasury finances. Initial framework will be developed in two stages.

This is actually a FinTech start up! And we MUST START NOW! Time is of the essence.

1. A kingdom treasury, A place to store wealth that minimizes effect of government and large bank control with blockchain linkages.

2. A private retail exchange where Kingdom individuals can trade and buy and sell without interference with full links to existing retail or neo-banking infrastructure for ATM.

The Favor Path
Analysis of the Kingdom Treasury drivers:
What is the problem to solve?

- The current financial system needs replacing.

- God's word says His people (those without the mark) will not be able to buy and sell produce.

- Philanthropists are disillusioned with Not-for profit/ donations sector without representation.

- Gods people want to do good in His Kingdom whilst retain their assets for future generations of their households.

- Good stewards want transparent and reliable information of where their funds are being used.

- Previous e-gold type systems didn't "know their customers". We will use the KYC and blockchain to secure transactions.

Who are those likely to be interested?

*Gods people who have made money from the worlds system by sweat of their brow and shrewd investments.

1. They may be disillusioned by poor experience in the "Christian" investment area in the past.

2. They can see the benefit of an "ARK" treasury in which to store their treasure / wealth, with less control of the antichristian forces (government, banks, or criminals).

3. They would like clear information on their fund value via system indicator and secure transactions.

4. They would like quick access (even via ATM) to a percentage of the funds and longer-term access to their legacy funds.

5. They are prepared to balance security of assets and receive a dividend return if they would like any of their funds used for projects.

6. They would like to participate in a kingdom endeavour to help fellow believers and build the body of Christ on earth (the bride ready for His return).

7. "Sophisticated investor" category Kingdom people who would like to pool God given assets for kingdom growth.

Covenant Relationships
Meaning The Parable of the Talents (Matthew 25:14-30) One of Jesus' most significant parables regarding work is set in the context of investments (Matt. 25:14-30). A rich man delegates the management of his wealth to his servants, much as investors in today's markets do. He gives five talents (a large unit of money) to the first servant, two talents to the second, and one talent to the third. Two of the servants earn 100 percent returns by trading with the funds, but the third servant hides the money in the ground and earns nothing. The rich man returns, rewards the two who made money, but severely punishes the servant who did nothing…..

The particular talent invested in the parable is money, on the order of a million U.S. dollars in today's world. In modern English, this fact is obscured because the word talent has come to refer mainly to skills or abilities. But this parable concerns money. It depicts investing, not hoarding, as a godly thing to do if it accomplishes godly purposes in a godly manner. In the end, the master praises the two trustworthy servants with the words, "Well done, good and trustworthy slave" (Matthew 25:23). In these words, we see that the master cares about the results ("well done"), the methods ("good"), and the motivation ("trustworthy")….

Alignment of Assignments
Scripture makes it clear that originally, there was only one kingdom – the Kingdom of God. Then, Lucifer (aka Satan) rebelled and was expelled from God's kingdom along with many angels. Since then, he has persistently sought to deceive men and women to join his kingdom – one that is characterized by disobedience and deceit.

Those who are loyal to God are challenged to help every person and every group on earth to recognize the opportunity to join the Kingdom of God. Choosing to believe the good news enables them to begin changing their world view. As faith takes root in our hearts, we can begin to appraise God's personal plans for us, to embrace those plans, and to pursue them. God's kingdom is characterized by trust, truth, peace, joy, and love – the opposite of

Satan's kingdom. "…to open their eyes, that they may turn from darkness to light and from the power of Satan unto God, that they may receive remission of sins and an inheritance among them that are sanctified by faith in me." Acts 26:18 ASV

Unfortunately, many of those with God's resources within our "Christendom" or body of Christ have been wounded by fellow Christian business owners in the past who have not fulfilled their agreement and honoured their investor brother/sisters. This has resulted in the kingdom funds being "invested" in the world system (currently belonging to Satan) and not God Kingdom.

For those who don't know, this is why the New Kingdom Global (NKG) was formed about six years ago to address the need. We plan to grow a new breed of kingdom companies that we can invest in with trust, that God can glorify Himself with and produce a multiplication of 30,60,100 fold without damaging them.

We may need to look at the best way to choose to allocate our funds which actually all belong to our father and creator. Many of the world systems and companies may have started out being honourable and sound then they were distorted and corrupted by the influences and deceptions of Satan without us realising.

Maybe we can learn and adapt ideas of trust from other groups such as the Jewish models and even the Islamic groups who have partly solved the problem for their communities?

Agreement and Collaboration
As part of the NKG community we established an initial review team that was formed as an advisory and candidates for part of the project team.

Abundance Economy Model
The treasury is at the center of the group of entities and forms the linkages between each of them. In the abundance economy the required funds would always be available for the kingdom investment by the kingprenuer, there would likely be a requirement for achievement of milestones and deliverables that benefit and grow the treasury and the whole Kingdom.

NKG Trade Exchange
Founded by Dr. Stan Jeffery 2016
The Kingdom Exchange (TKE)

We are introducing what we call "The Kingdom Exchange". This is to value everyone's contribution to each other's endeavours (jigsaw) and share in the returns. This includes using our networks and skills to find and connect people and groups who do not know and would never find each other without our networks. These concepts are well established in the world system as consultants, advisers, reviewers, and Intermediaries (IMs) with significant values and costs added to each project by their involvement.

The Kingdom Exchange would use a contribution recognition system with rewards based on future or current ability to pay and a "token based" measurement to register the actual values, and to see Christians flourishing in business by providing the means.

This would work together with a kingdom trading system where trust and integrity of product and services are required and valued.

The Favor Path
For many years, we have been seeking how to help Christians in business and TKE is the outcome of prayer and discernment. It was introduced to our boardroom prophets group who were supportive. It may be a little outside many Christians perspective, but I would ask you to make a cup of coffee and find a comfortable chair and relax and see if this is for you or your company to be involved in.

Word from God 4 April 2018 with regards to love for our brother and sisters: "If you spend all that you have on charities and do not have love for your brothers, then are you but a clanging cymbal"

Also in 1 John 3:16-18: "This is how we know what love is: Jesus Christ laid down his life for us. And we ought to lay down our lives for our brothers and sisters. If anyone has material possessions and sees a brother or sister in need but has no pity on them, how can the love of God be in that person? Dear children, let us not love with words or speech but with actions and in truth."

NKJV
Loving One Another 1 John 4: 21: "And he has given us this command: Those who love God must also love their Christian brothers and sisters". NLT

- Love is a doing word
- Do you have a need?
- What are you able to do for someone else?

Covenant Relationships
WHAT IS THE NEED AND THE OPPORTUNITY?

Have you ever wondered how the body of Christ should operate?

Many are realizing that the one hour on Sunday and occasional catch up in the week is not it?

Many God given ideas and projects are not sustained because we haven't sorted out the resourcing and funding. There is a tendency to say God will fix it. Well here is a solution that God has had us develop. We must bless each other with abundance because we are told to and not in the world's minimalist way.

Many of our saints and brothers/sisters are trapped in the world of poverty, lack and fear for the future. Our Lord and creator came to set us free as we implement His commands and requirements, one of which is to love (and serve) one another as He leads us.

TKE is one way we can serve and bless each other with our talents and gifts to build each other's business and dreams with an interlocking rewards system.

Alignment of Assignments
TKE matching process

The people/companies selected to join the exchange are
- Those needing assistance
- Those who provide the assistance
- Those who have and or need a product or service

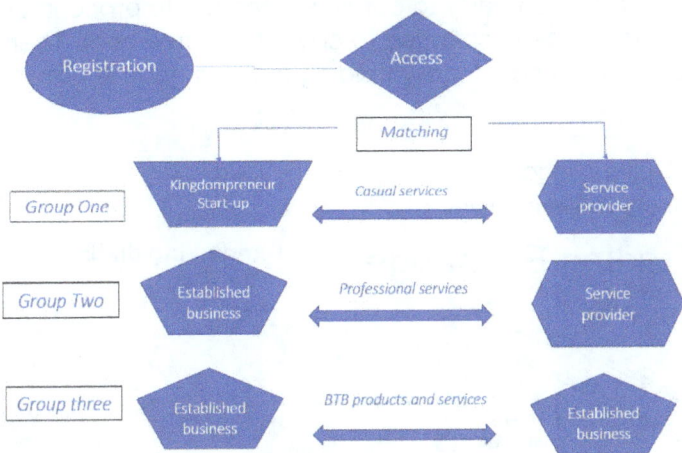

These are three basic transaction types of candidates
A). Those with needs that can be quantified and described.

- Those in this type must be able to provide a return for the services required
- This can be direct cash
- Equity if desired by the provider
- Revenue shares of returns
- Payment in other ways such as contra or barter

B). Those with skill and talents that are available to be used by those with a need
- This group must realistically value their contribution
- Need to consider new ways to be rewarded for their provision of services
- The fees may be accrued to be paid when the cash flow is available
- There may be a contra or barter need that can be provided directly to the recipient
- There may be a contra or barter need that can be provided directly to the TKE to rematch to others in the group
- The value of the fees is likely to be around $100 per hour.

C). Those with products and services that would benefit from increased / international exposure in the Kingdom networks.

The TKE engine and matching process will (when completed) attempt to provide a likely match. This will be reviewed by the TKE staff.

This will be supplied to each party to obtain agreement to proceed and then the legal documents will be exchanged to cover the agreement. There will be a confidentially agreement and a legally binding contract for the provision or use of services.

Agreement and Collaboration
Who are those likely to be involved?

NKG Trading Exchange — Interlinking diagram

```
                         TKE
        10%                              10%
              1 TKE token
              Introduction reward
                    10 TKE tokens
                    Plus 2 TKE tokens
                         10%
   Company A  ←──────────────────────→  Company C
                      5K cash
              5K cash         5K cash
   10 TKE tokens                    10 TKE tokens
   Plus 2 TKE tokens                Plus 1 TKE tokens
                      Company B
```

Note 1 TKE token is equivalent to $500

- Those in the kingdom of God are believers and those outside are unbelievers. This is agreed by most people, even Christians
- Those who believe are also those who fear (revere and glorify) the Creator God
- They do not need worldly rules and contracts. They just need to believe that God is with them and
- They are with Him in all things and
- Agree with each other under God's covenant agreements

Abundance Economy Model
TKE is here to help you build a Kingdom business with trustworthy skilled kingdom staff to match your every need!

We have all wished that we could quickly find the sort of people "like us" with similar values and vision. The growing of business that honour God and extend His kingdom is generally what many people aspire to and many mission statements would support this. To see Christians flourishing in kingdom business by providing the means for them to receive the assistance required

- Provide systems for Christians to invest time and resource in each other
- Increase the potency of marketplace Christians
- A place goods and services can be converted to cash
- Promote Christians businesses…their Kingdom purpose
- Protect the church organisations from any involvement with failing business dealings

Allegheny River Retreat Center
Founded by Kevin and Tami Barthen 2017

Vision

• It is only through understanding who we truly are that we can begin to understand who we are able to become. Man's relationship with their Creator was broken and as a result mankind has been blind to their true identity and purpose. Because of this broken relationship, our relationships with one another have been a poor representation of what our Creator truly intended and without an authentic relationship with our Creator, we wander aimlessly through the earth lost – never coming into the true knowledge of who we are and settling for whatever our mere minds can determine for our lives, but there is so much more available to us!

• Through Christ, man has been restored and given all they need to be reconciled to God. In Him, through Christ, our identity is discovered, our relationships with one another become rooted and grounded in honor and respect, and we become empowered to fulfill our destiny in the earth – we live out our purpose. A divine plan has been specifically designed just for you.

• At ARRC we will provide an environment designed for individuals, families, groups and corporations to discover their true identity, develop strong healthy covenantal relationships, and become empowered to fulfill their commission in the earth.

Mission Statement

• Nestled in the quiet hills of the Allegheny Mountains of Western Pennsylvania, the Allegheny River Retreat Center (ARRC) provides a **unique setting** for a time of refreshment and recreation away from the hustle and bustle of daily life.

- Our Mission is to create **year-round opportunities** and activities for individuals, families, groups and corporations to discover their multifaceted identity, and **develop relationships** with one another that are rooted in honor and respect, empowering them to fulfill their designed commission.

- ARRC offers several activities designed around different types of interests. Our workshops are designed to help individuals, families, groups and corporations **discover their true identity**. The ultimate goal of every workshop is for them to discover how they were designed and who they were meant to be.

- Relationships are enhanced by **shared experiences**. Our recreational programs will facilitate shared experiences between individuals, families, groups and corporations.

- **Nature** surrounds our campus giving it beauty and an easy place to feel the **presence of peace**. The awe-inspiring view on the overlook and the natural beauty of ARRC will facilitate the relationship between individuals and their Creator.

- Our outdoor recreation gives groups, the young, and the young at heart, a place to **play, explore, and enjoy** the glory of creation. Direct access to the river, scenic hiking trails, and a host of other amenities are all special qualities of ARRC.

- ARRC will be opening several of the amenities to the public to impact their personal lives and facilitate **community goodwill.**

Project Definition

- A.R.R.C. is envisioned as a **Christian response to the daily stressors in our work and personal lives**. This retreat center is committed to helping people understand their relationship with Christ and to reveal tools that help them to be more successful in their daily lives. The center is a respite from daily stressors, a place to re-center, rest and revive.
- Build a **retreat center** for churches, businesses, groups and families to attend from all over the country.
- Bring in world renowned speakers to share their message.
- Create a space for **education, spiritual, wellness, safety and team building.**
- Provide a destination for weddings, conferences and family functions.
- Create jobs for Venango County and surrounding counties.
- Increasing tourism for all local establishments.
- **Provide fresh grown produce** (in cooperation with Abundance Farms) for the camp attendees, local markets and e-commerce.

Project Attributes

Benefits
• Jobs Created **80-90**

• The Business Plan projects profits. The plan is to turn 30% of those profits into Local ministries, Samaritans Purse and The Passion Translation and other nonprofit organizations.

• The Business Plan projects self-sustaining at 30 months.

• Social: ARRC provides beautiful indoor and outdoor space for leadership training and conferences for businesses and churches

and individuals. The setting is perfect for friend and family gatherings such as parties, weddings and reunions.

• Environmental: Hydroponic gardens are just one of the ways the environment will benefit from ARRC, through the sustainability of self-grown nutrient rich foods.

• Economic: Not only will the town benefit from the increased jobs that ARRC will provide but the local merchants will thrive with the added tourism brought on by ARRC.

• Spiritual problem solved: ARRC will provide the perfect space for people to rest, reset, reconnect and refresh spiritually. With the outstanding guest speakers and teachers to the amazing Christian concerts, there will be plenty of opportunity to recharge.

Stewardship
• ARRC, a for profit entity, will have profit sharing with managers and employees.

• A portion of profits will also support Samaritan's Purse and The Passion Translation.

• 80-90 jobs are created in a depressed community.

• ARRC will be working with local university programs and providing work-study opportunities.

• The Abundance Farm Greenhouse on ARRC property will provide nutrient dense food for the retreat center, local grocers and through e-commerce.

• Engage professional RGT/ GMP mentorship/ guidance in development and operation of the Retreat Center.

Number and Location of Units to be Deployed

• The ARRC Retreat center in Franklin, Pennsylvania is the main focus for this project. It has been prophesied that this center would stand as a model for others across the country and world.

Abundance Economy Model

A Community Corporation which act as a hybrid with characteristics of both sustaining profit generating entities and community serving entities. ARRC will use their products or services instead of cash profits for providing food, water, housing and education for their community mission. ARRC will still provide well-paying jobs and reward sharing for management and employees while demonstrating the ability to Pay It Forward with products and services to the community and support new Pay It Forward entities.

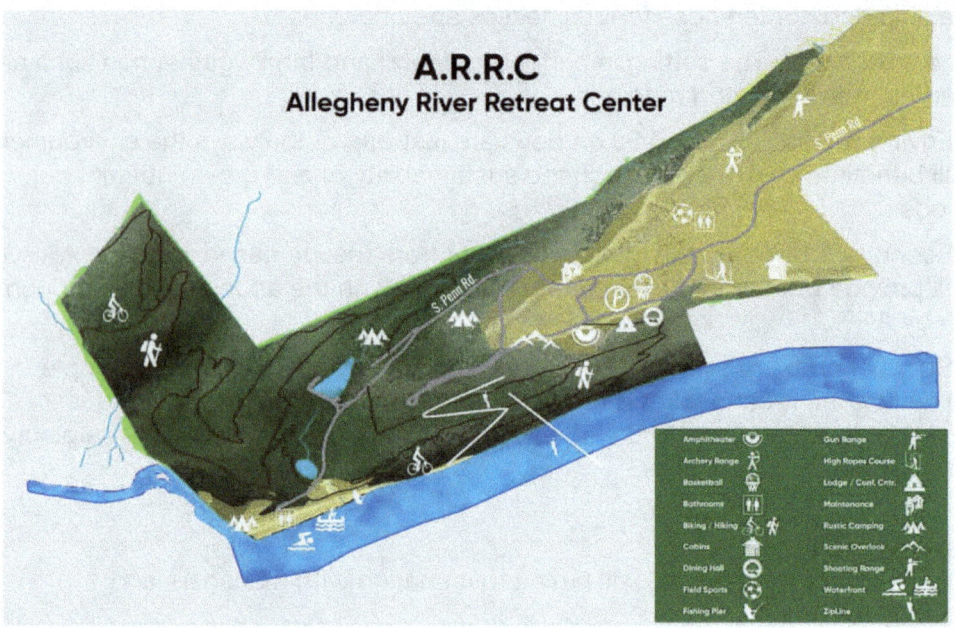

Kingdom of Christ University
Founded by Dr. William Hinn, Drs. Mark and Jill Kauffman 2020

Vision Statement

The church has done well preparing people to go to Heaven but has failed to prepare the people of God to influence and impact their world. The Biblical foundations of our present educational systems are deteriorating rapidly. We must reclaim education by developing Kingdom schools and universities with a Biblical worldview that will empower students to engage the world and influence it with the culture of Heaven. Our goal must be to prepare our generation with Biblical truths that will empower them to engage the culture and influence every sphere of society. Our culture is shaped by the seven mountains of cultural influence: business, government, media, arts/entertainment, education, family, and religion.

By raising up a new breed of servant leaders, they will be trained and equipped to become change agents in our present culture so they can demonstrate the Kingdom of God in the world in which they live. With a global perspective, present day truth, and excellence demonstrated in the art of teaching, Kingdom of Christ University (KCU) will prepare its students to advance the Lord's purposes in the earth.

KCU's vision is to raise up echelon leaders who are well prepared and seasoned to lead the next season in God's Kingdom reformation and community revitalization. KCU's curriculum empowers churches to become training centers and apostolic/prophetic epicenters in their communities. We can no longer continue to teach people how to maintain their salvation, but rather give them the equipping tools to demonstrate their salvation in their personal spheres of influence. The world has viewed the church as a place of lonely, weak, ignorant, and uneducated people. Through KCU, we recover the true essence of the church becoming the answer to worldly problems as salt and light to this present world. KCU's curriculum is a Kingdom template that leads its students into a deeper, more intimate relationship with their Heavenly Father and prepares them to thrive at the top of their sphere. Through the Kingdom of Christ University, we are committed to raising up a new breed of leaders who will reclaim the earth for King Jesus.

Curriculum Development

The scope of these services includes:

(1) Development of core curriculum for KCU degree programs. The curriculum will be developed in either an on-line or hybrid format and compatible with KCU's choice of Learning Management System. At the course level this will include title, description, prerequisites, objectives, and required methods of assessment, outline of topics, cognitive levels met, and core attributes met. Course level documentation must be delivered in the KCU Course Content Outline format.

(2) Provide program and course design, delivery and implementation assistance. Working with KCU faculty and staff, this activity should include: identifying options for course content delivery, determining course values (possible credits, lab hours and theory hours), performing (where appropriate) an analysis of KCU course materials for content or design/implement new ones; that align with the completion of the program's certificates and degrees.

LMS: A *learning management system* is a software application for the administration, documentation, tracking, reporting, and delivery of educational courses, training programs, or learning and development programs. The learning management system concept emerged directly from e-Learning.

Blackboard ~ Desire 2 Learn ~ Jenzabar One ~ Canvas ~ Moodle ~ LearnDash

CMS: A *content management system* is a software application that can be used to manage the creation and modification of digital content. CMSs are typically used for enterprise content management and web content management. Professors and department heads can update their department webpages by themselves.

Your institution's website is your greatest marketing and recruitment asset, but managing it is no small feat.

Omni Update ~ Ingenieux ~ Hannon Hill ~ LiveWhale ~ Jadu ~ WordPress

SIS: *Student Information System* (or SIS) is the core of any educational institution. It helps to manage student data. These systems store and process large amounts of personal and critical data (e.g. payment information, medical records of current and former students and employees, class schedule, grades, etc.).

Banner ~ PeopleSoft Campus Solution ~ **Jenzabar SONIS** ~ Salesforce for Education ~ College by Ellucian

Infrastructure: This consists of all the hardware, fiberoptic cabling and CAT6 cabling. The infrastructure equipment will supply data transport across the network and to the cloud-based services employed. Each student, faculty and staff member will utilize these services, even while taking online courses from the campus and teaching online courses from faculty offices.

Physical University

Custodial, facility management, grounds maintenance, HVAC maintenance, and general maintenance will be outsourced. Custodians and general maintenance employees will be employees of the contractor.

- The physical university contractor will provide ongoing building maintenance, janitorial and groundskeeping services, and manage utility costs associated with maintaining a facility.
- A new facility will require a major renovation approximately every 30 years given the life cycles for HVAC and electrical systems, advances in technology, and deterioration of building structures such as roofs, windows, doors, and building envelope. Due to the new construction and installation of new systems within the KCU building these are costs that can be effectively managed.

The cost estimate includes salaries and benefits, maintenance and custodial equipment services and supplies, energy and utility costs, grounds-keeping and general maintenance costs.

Security Firm

Estimated costs for security services are based on the average cost for security services in the region and include:

- Direct salaries and benefits for security personnel assigned to KCU for supervisors/management, security guards. ***We estimate needing an onsite Director/Supervisor and 4 officers; 3 fulltime and 1 part time***
- Benefits afforded to the security guards, health, dental, sick pay, holiday pay, pension, and paid time off
- Administrative costs and proposed profit
- Equipment and one-time start-up costs

Security services will include, maintaining order, deterring intrusion, resolution of disputes, deterrence of violence, theft and vandalism, providing reception, assistance, information, responding to emergencies and submitting regular daily reports including incident and facility condition reports.

All security personnel will be employees of the Contractor. The Contractor will be responsible for the hiring, training, equipping, supervising, directing, and discharging of the Security Personnel. The Contractor will be responsible for the payment of all Federal, State, and local taxes and overtime wages.

Medical Services

Our onsite medical services will provide an onsite CRNP 2 days a week and an RN 3 days a week.

The primary care of a nurse practitioner and/or nursing staff until further medical assistance can be provided by a physician

- An active Health Promotion Department focusing on education, prevention and nutrition services
- Provide referrals to counseling and psychological services, including crisis visits
- Compliance with all legal health requirements such as immunizations
- Student outreach programs such as free flu shots and other activities to keep the campus safe and to respond to community health issues as they arise

- The availability of an on-campus Health Services Department assures confidentiality for all students, provides easy, convenient access to health care, and allows for minimal disruption to student academic activities.

We would like to thank you for the opportunity to present our vision for developing a new educational blueprint that will raise up a new breed of servant-leaders to be trained and equipped to become change agents in our present culture.

The culture, curriculum, and environment created within Kingdom of Christ University will defy a world, dominated by fear and greed, enabling its students to demonstrate that the impossible is possible.

Again, thank you for this wonderful opportunity and your consideration in this matter is greatly appreciated.

Abundance Economy Model: A Community Corporation which act as a hybrid with characteristics of both sustaining profit generating entities and community serving entities. KCU will use their products or services instead of cash profits for providing food, housing and education for their community mission. KCU will still provide well-paying jobs and reward sharing for management and employees while demonstrating the ability to Pay It Forward with products and services to the community and support new Pay It Forward entities.

Focus Life Institute
Founded by Dr. Ed Turose 2016

eturose@focuslifeinstitute.com

Personal Info • I am 64 years old and currently reside in Grove City, PA • I am married to my wife Cindy for 43 years and have 2 children and 3 grandchildren

Divine Assignment • I have been given the assignment to equip and help this generation and generations to come to get focused to fulfill their purpose, assignment and destiny in life. After spending over 37 years in Fortune 500, I retired early to fulfill my assignment. •

Personal Story: I was saved when I was 13 and have served God all my life. However, in 1988, I received the baptism of the Holy Spirit and began my journey to advance God's Kingdom. In 1995, after being downsized, I fasted and prayed for a week and God told me that I would be able to change generations and get them focused to achieve their God-given destiny. Since that time, I have invested my time, talent and treasure to advance God's Kingdom in this assignment.

Preparation and Experience for Assignment S.B.A. 1977 Geneva College, Beaver Falls, PA
Unilever Regional Manager – 10 Years 1977 - 1987
The Coca-Cola Company - 27 years as a Senior National Account Manager, Trainer and Manager of a $75 Million Territory 1987 – 1995, 1998 – 2017
Certified Behavioral Consultant in the DISC Behavioral System (1992) and Creator of Career Quest Educational and Retention Program 1995 – 1998
Doctor of Divinity from Tabernacle Bible College
Associate Professor – Geneva College Business Department
Author of 3 books and multiple e-courses in education, business, and recovery
Consultant, Coach, Trainer and Strategic Planner for businesses
President of the Christian Chamber of Commerce of Western Pennsylvania
Elder at Jubilee Ministries International City Church
Focus Life TV Program – Faith Unveiled TV Network and focusEDtalk Weekly Podcast Chief Administrative Officer at Global Impact Mega Corporation

I serve in the following capacity:
President, Christian Chamber of Commerce of Western PA
Elder, Jubilee Ministries International Church and NOW Project
Served on board of Global Impact Mega Corporation
Elder in 2 other churches, worship leader, Caregroup (small group) Leader and Overseer

The Focus Life Institute

Mission: to educate, equip and empower individuals to focus on identifying their assignment and calling, achieving their purpose and fulfilling their destiny in life. We are a training and development company that delivers practical online courses offering the skills needed to achieve greater levels of productivity and success in life.

We help unlock your potential in the areas of personal and professional development, by offering curriculums, FastTrack courses, and specific modules designed around the key areas of vocational spheres of influence, business, education, career readiness, essential skills development, workplace preparation, values/character development and recovery/reentry.

Our Fast track business modules are focused on providing competence in organizational and relational effectiveness in the workplace. We offer essential and employable skills training that increases productivity, profitability and efficiency. Our values and character development model, entitled the Heroes Effect, provides the training of the lost values in our current society: honor, excellence, responsibility, order, expectation, and servant hood.

The Focus Life Institute provides educational curriculum for grades K-12, colleges, universities and organizational groups focusing on career readiness and workplace preparation. In the area of recidivism and re-entry, we offer materials that will help individuals overcome personal setbacks by gaining the skills they need to be effective in the workplace. In addition, we also offer our modules in a faith-based option.

What is the problem?

Educational Challenges
- An estimated 20 to 50 percent of students enter a post-secondary education experience without declaring a major course of study. Source: Gordon

- Over 80% of students change their major course of study at least 1 to 3 times with an average cost of over $12,000 per change. Source: National Center of Education Statistics

- Over 50% of students are not working a job or career in their major course of study. This is a waste of time and money if you are not working in a job or career based on your time and financial investment. Source: CareerBuilder

- 55% of students do not feel positively about their college and career readiness. Source: YouthTruth

- Over 30% of students drop out of college within the first two years. Source: National Student Clearinghouse and the Organization of Economic Cooperation and Development

- The average retention rate for colleges is 72% with most schools losing millions of dollars annually. Workplace Challenges

- Due to workplace distractions, businesses are losing millions of dollars annually. Over 70% of workers admit they feel distracted when they are on the job. Source: Udemy, Workplace Distraction Report

- According to CareerBuilder.com, the following are the top distraction areas in our daily lives: cell phones, texting, emails, gossip, Internet surfing, social media, snack breaks, noisy co-workers, meetings, and co-workers dropping by.

- For over the past 20 years, employers continue to say that graduates coming out of college, university or technical schools continued to lack the soft skills to be able to be successful within their company or organization. Source: PayScale

- According to LinkedIn's "Workplace Learning Report," soft skills are the No. 1 priority for talent development. Further, a LinkedIn study found that hiring managers indicated their company's productivity was limited due to a lack of candidates' soft skills. Findings by the Stanford Research Institute International and the Carnegie Mellon Foundation found that 75% of long-term job success depends upon soft skills mastery and only 25% of technical skills.

- "The No. 1 problem with today's young workforce is the soft skills gap. It runs across the entire workforce – among workers with technical skills that are in great demand, every bit as much as workers without technical skills. Soft skills are key to individuals' success in the workplace and are a competitive differentiator in the marketplace. They're the source of a huge amount of power that is always right there hiding in plain sight – a tremendous reservoir of often untapped value – a secret weapon for any smart organization, team, leader or individual performer." – Bruce Tulgan

- A lack of FOCUS is why many people fail. We live in an age of distractions! Our attention spans now last under 8 seconds! Each of us are being constantly interrupted by distractions every day. Recovery/Reentry Challenges

- Overall Recidivism: For offenders age 24 or younger at the time of release, 63.2 percent of federal prisoners were rearrested within five years compared to over four-fifths (84.1%) of state prisoners.

- College Graduates and Recidivism: Among offenders under age 30 at the time of release, college graduates had a substantially lower re-arrest rate (27.0%) than offenders who did not complete high school (74.4%)

- The majority of inmates have minimal, if any, job or career training.

What is the solution?

I am proposing that the Focus Life Institute focuses on equipping and training students within the New Castle, PA area and extending services within our region. Focus Life e-courses have been tested in high schools, junior high schools, and college courses. As a trainer for Fortune 500, I have utilized these materials of the behavioral profiles with The Coca-Cola Company and its food broker, Acosta Sales and Marketing.

The following e-courses have been created and ready now to be deployed into the educational arenas, reentry and workplace development arenas. Listed below are our current e-courses.

Finding Life's Direction: Our Finding Life's Direction e-course will provide you with a process to get focused on your career path to be prepared for your future. The e-Course is an all-inclusive practical development tool based on your personal behavioral style. Sessions include Vision, Personality, Passion, Profession and Peak Performance. Our e-course is online and includes personalized profiles, videos, PDF's, note-taking ability, exams, facilitator guides and a course certificate.

Skills for Success: In this lesson, we will utilize your personal DISC behavioral style and provide you with the following top 10 skills.

- People Skills (Adaptability/Flexibility)
- Time management - Communication
- Collaboration
- Conflict Resolution
- Creativity
- Confidence
- Decision-making
- Problem-solving
- Values and Character
- Bonus: Interviewing skills

This course will produce the following outcomes:

- Gained an understanding of the different behavioral styles and the motivations of others to communicate more effectively.

- Identify the ways to improve in your personal time management

- Learned How to Increase Communicate More Effectively With Different Behavioral Styles

- Discovered How To Collaborate More Efficiently Within a Team Concept

- Pinpointed Ways to Reduce and Resolve Conflict Between Team Members
- Uncovered Your Qualities of Creativity That Can Be Utilized in the Workplace
- Identified Your Behavioral Traits Producing Confidence in the Workplace
- Acquired the critical thinking skills of problem solving and decision-making
- Recognized How To Protect Your Character
- Be Equipped on the Behavioral Interview to Secure Your Desired Job

HEROES - Values and Character Development: The HEROES Effect helps students identify what specific virtues they need to improve on to be effective in the workplace. Included are practical applications for each virtue and personal stories with related results. Applying these virtues will produce favor with their managers and peers, increase in opportunities for their advancement and influence to those within their personal and professional life. The acronym of the 6 virtues include: Honor, Excellence, Responsibility, Order, Expectation, and Servanthood.

In addition, we offer the following:

K-12 public/private schools, homeschool 36 week educational curriculum

College and university courses for retention and workplace preparation

Professional Development Courses include:
- Overcoming Workplace Distractions
- Customer Focused Sales Strategies
- Essential Soft Skills
- Personal and Behavioral Development
- HEROES Leadership

The Focus Life Institute E-courses include the following:
- Online e-learning
- Personalized Profiles
- Individual Sessions
- Creative Videos
- Interactive PDF's with Questions
- Personal Note Taking and Reflection
- Facilitator Video and Training Guides
- 2 E-books: The Focus Fulfilled Life and The Heroes Principle

Who Benefits? How?

- Increase retention for colleges and reentrants
- Understand vision, purpose and assignment - most people lack vision
- Discover a career path - Over 50% of students are not working in their major
- Save time and money - Over 80% change their major 1-3 times costing $12k/change
- Identify your sphere or mountain of influence
- Create a lifestyle of focus and overcome distractions
- Secure your desired job with the Behavioral Interviewing Techniques
- Raise achievement levels - focusing helps you achieve your goals and objectives
- Acquire values and character development for advancement in the workplace
- Equip and train business leaders for the future to influence society

The students in our pilot programs have enjoyed our courses. Here are a few responses:
It was a fun and enjoyable experience for our students who were able to connect with real-life application that fit their personality and potential career choices. Students enjoyed the material followed by a hands-on, energetic activity that allowed them to interact with other students. Unlike other inventories, students connected with the real-life application and fit to their personality and potential career choices. Students thoroughly enjoyed the implanted videos within the lessons; these media break-up the monotony of a full lecture period. Kristen Richards, Guidance Counselor, Greenville Junior High School, Greenville, PA (Blue Ribbon School in Pa) Pilot Program.

I feel like the skills that were taught are valuable and apply to the workplace. In school we are mainly taught the X's and O's and not taught how to deal with people. I have had a couple of interviews since learning about the DISC and people skills training, and I was able to easily identify their personalities. It helped me in the interviewing process, by giving me a feel on what they wanted to know from the interview. Overall, I believe these skills are very essential when I get out into the workplace and deal with people daily. D.R. Geneva College, Beaver Falls, PA.

Mr. Turose, thank you so much for investing into my life this semester and teaching us all the super important life skills that we won't find in our textbooks. Learning how to get in sync with others is so important in all our relationships. Thank you so much for teaching us how to do that. The skills you have taught us in this class are so beneficial and I thank you for bringing all your real-life experiences in during the class. Also, thank you for making this class fun. I really enjoyed this class, but I don't think I would have enjoyed as much with a different professor. J. M. Geneva College, Beaver Falls, PA.

Course Implementation

- Dr. Turose, as a manager and trainer with The Coca-Cola Company, trained multiple regions across the country with these developmental tools
- These courses were used at Eastern University during a study on increasing retention
- Dr. Turose taught students as an adjunct professor at Geneva College, Beaver Falls, PA
- These courses have been utilized in high schools for career readiness and workplace preparation
- The 32-session Career and Workplace Preparation course is currently being offered at the International School of Ministry (isom.org) and offered to their 250,000 students across the world

drive.google.com/file/d/14YZpFQVkDWzetfwuaiueAL5QA mFocXAz/view

Your Focus Determines Your Future!

Abundance Economy Model
A Community Corporation which act as a hybrid with characteristics of both sustaining profit generating entities and community serving entities. FLI will use their products or services instead of cash profits for providing education for their community mission. FLI will still provide well-paying jobs and reward sharing for management and employees while demonstrating the ability to Pay It Forward with products and services to the community and support new Pay It Forward entities.

Dynamis World Industries
Founded by Thomas Meade 2020

What is the Problem?

- Furniture and furnishings made with particle board and fabrics which exposes both workers and customers to toxic and unhealthy chemicals, and uses nonrenewable resources.

What is the Solution?

- The Dynamis Micro-factory Model

- *A World-wide Solution to Help Promote Community Sustainability*

- A highly efficient, high-margin furniture manufacturing template reverse engineered for 30 years from a Kingdom perspective and sustainable focus to serve the needs of People, Communities and the Environment that is nearly ready to expand globally.

- A unique, scalable, low-capital manufacturing model focused on taking local, renewable resources to provide affordable, functional and essential living space needs for virtually every dwelling on the planet that creates a wide range of jobs at nearly every skill level while focusing on the health and wealth of the employees and the community.

- With a further goal of being THE community model to promote food, health and energy independence as the world's first bio-dynamically integrated manufacturer where every output is an input for something else - zero waste and carbon negative.

- It's not about furniture, it's about the Way you chose to live. There is the World's Way and then there is A Better Way, GOD'S WAY.

What does a "Solution" look like?

Dynamis company, products and vision are the creation of Thomas Lee Meade, a Penn State Mechanical Engineering graduate (BSME '87). Having recognized a need for affordable, solid-wood furniture at the time and possessing an insatiable desire to create and innovate, the company was started in 1989 in a 140+ year old barn with a 200 sq ft store. That led to a facility with three buildings with 28,000 sq ft, a 4000 sq ft retail store, multiple websites and products sold nationally and internationally via many channels.

The focus has always been to provide innovative, functional furnishings at an affordable price produced with the least environmental impact. Since this paradox didn't exist, it had to be created. Thus the focus on an eco-friendly product line using fast growing, highly- sustainable Southern Yellow Pine with virtually no waste by-products (clean sawdust is sold for bedding and wood scraps recycled for burning). The goal is to eventually be 100% energy independent and to set the pace for the industry through product, process and business model innovation - the FIRST BioDynamically Integrated Manufacturer in America.

- The company is at the forefront of the future of the furniture industry, a vertically-integrated, multi-channel manufacturer selling direct to end users with the ability to offer complete, a turn-key furniture solutions - furniture and bedding direct to consumers, retailers, government agencies, institutions or large end users. The future of manufacturing in the 21st century is mass-customization distributed via company stores supported by a strong, web-based e-Commerce platform. We hope to lead this in a sustainable way.

- In summary, as a proud supplier of *"THE Most Affordable, Solid-wood, Eco-friendly Furniture in America,"* along with a focus on *"Simple, Healthy Living"* solutions inside and outside the home, our vision is to become the nation's first vertically integrated "Sustainable Lifestyle Store" brand, supported by our manufacturing, retailing, e-Commerce and distribution capabilities. By aligning ourselves with the wants and needs of society, in the present and future age, we believe this is the future of 21st century capitalism.

PRODUCTS MANUFACTURED: Solid-wood

• Innovative Futon Frames Platform Beds & Captain's Bed Bunk Beds & Loft Beds

• Futon Bunk Bed Convertibles Bookshelves & Entertainment Centers

• Case goods (night stands, dressers & chests, media stands, underbed storage, coffee tables

• Various Other Furniture Accessories (ladders, clip-on shelves, snack trays, foot-stools)

CAPABILITIES:

• Design & Manufacture solid wood, eco-friendly furniture from Southern Yellow Pine and Pennsylvania Red Oak that is easy to assemble and ship flat (flat packed/RTA)

• Eco-friendly Finishes: Low-VOC water-based dip tanks & water-based nano-polymer spraying

• Turnkey Furniture Solutions - mainly bedrooms & living rooms, with some dining rooms

• Affordable bedding, mattresses and futons available

• Custom Sizes for Special Applications - Twin XL, Full XL, custom height, custom lengths, etc.

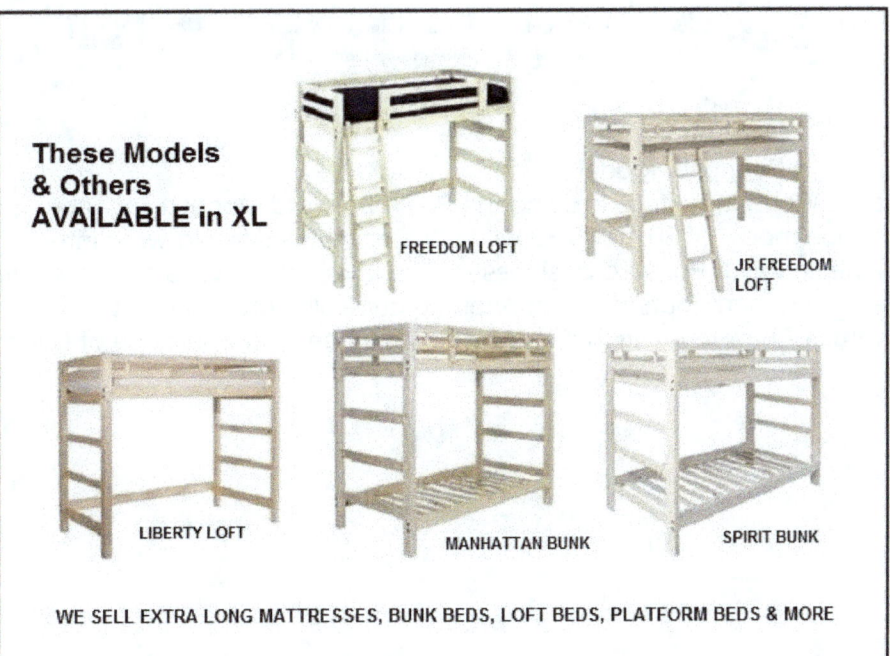

Abundance Economy Model
Dynamis World Industries is using the Pay It Forward Model using a profit dispersion model of 30:10:30:30 with 30% being invested forward into sustainable Pay It Forward businesses. The IP developed is also shared with participating, contributing and supporting our Collaborators that they may grow fruit of new innovations and technologies beyond the scope of Dynamis World Industries.

New Life Abundance Training Centre
Founded by Roelie Etsebeth 2020

About seven years ago God began to speak to me about education. It sort of sounds strange as we are living in an age where technology is on the rise and knowledge is increasing at a rapid rate. Yet at the same time we find ourselves with a society that is in many ways declining. The gap between the rich and the poor is widening and many of the basic skills are disappearing.

At our church we started feeding the homeless that were increasing in our area. Many of these homeless people did not finish school and besides the fact that they grew up poor. They never had the opportunity to be taught a skillset, had lack of money, had lack of guidance, had wrong friends etc. also plays it part. Now they are finding themselves in a world where they must survive with little or no help to further themselves in life. In many countries I see the same thing over and over again that the general thought is that these people made their choices, and they have to live with it. If the Word of God says that God's people are destroyed by a lack of knowledge, we are literally seeing it playing out in front of our eyes as "innocent" bystanders. I believe that the Church has not yet seen this enormous place of evangelism and abundance that can be unfolded in the Kingdom of God. I am reminded by the Grace of God sending His Son that we may have life and have it more abundantly. The more people that have life the more God's abundance will be evident in our lives.

So many people's lives are destroyed because of bad circumstances at home including the lack of a father figure who is the resource or distributor of the life and abundance of God. The Church must take its place as the distributor of the Grace and Abundance of God. One of the key factors is that we have to minister not only to the spirit man, but also to the Soul and the body. We have seen over the years most Christian's leave Church on Sunday feeling refreshed and revitalized, only to be in fear and dread on a Monday because they have not been equipped to live from day to day. The vision of New Life Abundance will be to train people with a practical skill, like for example plumbing/ electrical/ programming/ accounting/ building/ project management etc. A farming skill cultivating their own vegetables and equipping them with biblical principles to live a Kingdom lifestyle, therefore addressing three areas of their man.

This is not a be all and end all, but a start to what I believe will set off a powerful movement to empower the Church that the sons of God, (plural) will be manifested. For the whole of creation is awaiting, groaning for the sons to take back their place. How will they know if someone doesn't tell and teach them His ways. Universities will follow that will not teach our young in the ways of this world, but in the ways of Gods Kingdom.

What is the Problem?
- The problem is the high unemployment prevalent in South Africa
- Unemployment rate of 29%, unofficial rate 40%
- Youth unemployment – age group 15 – 24 – 55%

What is the Solution?
- How does it solve the problem?
- Skills development
- Training of artisans, horticulture, self-sustainable small scale farming, small business development, basic computer skills
- Practical Experience
- Strong emphasis would also be on the impartation of the Word of God and a Kingdom mindset
- Two tier basis - Christ centered training curriculum, bible classes or a bible school
- Discipleship

What is the Solution?
- Is the Technology Proprietary?
- Some of the technology might be under license such as the computer software to be used for soft skills training
- Who benefits? How? How much?
- Students – personal upliftment, self-worth, skills impartation, family impact, health. Spiritual impartation
- Broader community – skills and spiritual impact. Health and economic
- Church & surrounding areas – involvement in projects and community upliftment, spiritual and social
- Cost and time per to deploy

Project Solution Attributes
- Investment Timeline
- 9 – 12 Months (Stage 1)
- Time from Operation to self-sustaining or steady-state funds flow?
- 12 Months
- Benefits
- Job Created
- 5 -10 permanent jobs (Staff)

- Money Generated
- Produce from crops, artisan and creative projects
- Does it become self-sustaining? How and when?
  - By selling crops / produce, crafts. Stage 1 – 12 months
- Other Social / Environmental / Economic / Spiritual problems solved
- Poverty relief, community upliftment, spiritual impartation with possible church planting, evangelization. Job creation

Project Solution Attributes

- Stewardship – that all may prosper
- How do managers and employees participate in profits (or operating surplus, if Nonprofit)
- Operating Surplus is ploughed back into projects for equipment, consumables, daily running of projects, expansion on longer term projects (Stage 2 & 3), salaries etc.
- How do the communities where the Solution is delivered benefit?
- Spiritual impartation / change
- Making poor communities self-sustainable – economic betterment
- Health & mental benefits
- Possible job creation

Number and Location of Units to be Deployed

- Map(s) and / or List of Locations, if known
- IF not known, state basis of decision for estimating the number to be deployed
- Proposed site have been identified in the centre of area of church influence, that is close to main traffic arteries that can easily be accessed by relevant recipients. The property is big enough to host several projects at the same time

Pace:

- Schedule of number deployed per year over some project horizon
- (Stage 1) Training course for vegetable gardens will be approximately 4 months or one vegetable season. (Roughly 20 – 30 persons per course = 60 / 90 per year for the first year – Pilot project)
- (Stage 2) Computer skills, small business training. 10 over period of 2 months - 60 per year for first year
- (Stage 3) Training of artisans – Up to stage 2 – approximately 2 months. 5 – 10 persons – 30 / 60 per year

Abundance Economy Model

A Community Corporation which act as a hybrid with characteristics of both sustaining profit generating entities and community serving entities. NLATC will use their products or services instead of cash profits for providing education for their community mission. NLATC will still provide well-paying jobs and reward sharing for management and employees while demonstrating the ability to Pay It Forward with products and services to the community and support new Pay It Forward entities.

Regulus Energy, LLC
Founded in 2012 by Glenn Thomas, CEO
glenn.thomas@regulus.energy

PROVIDING ALTERNATIVE ENERGY FOR TODAY'S NEEDS

The vision of Regulus Energy is to serve God and Man by providing environmentally sound, cost effective renewable technologies to nations to solve critical problems, improve the quality of life, build diversified economies and help them move towards energy independence by converting waste streams into fuels, chemicals and electricity.

Regulus systems convert a variety of carbon feedstocks including municipal solid waste (MSW), wood, energy crops, plants, sewage, plastics, natural gas and coal into cost-effective production of renewable fuels including methanol, ethanol and butanol, and hydrocarbon fuels – jet fuel and diesel. Electricity generation and chemicals are also proven and viable options. Building on world-leading proprietary technologies including steam reforming, Fischer Tropsch and pyrolysis proven over years of use in demonstration and production plants, Regulus personnel have over 150 years of combined experience in the alternative energy sector and extensive EPC and training experience. The company possesses a strong base of know-how and IP. The plant and operating experience of Regulus technologies exceeds 70 years.

Currently Regulus is working to commercialize multiple US and foreign projects. These initial projects will use MSW or wood as the feedstock with diesel #2, jet fuel, ethanol or methanol as the offtake product. The MSW plants will take in garbage otherwise destined for landfills, reducing the landfill volume by 80% or more while producing advanced cellulosic fuels that meet ASTM specifications – jet fuel (ASTM D7566, D1655) and ultra-low sulfur diesel #2 (ASTM D975) with exceptionally clean combustion efficiencies, methanol (ASTM D1152 and D5797) or ethanol (ASTM D4806 and D5798). These renewable fuels are in high demand worldwide and are readily sold through a variety of offtake options. The plants produce essentially zero emissions and will employ from 60 to over 250 people per site depending on plant capacity. Plant capacities range from 25 million to 475 million gallons of fuel annually. The plants are profitable without subsidy and generate strong EBITDA and ROI.

The following information further describes the current problems with management of MSW and other waste streams, the use of crude based fuels, and the solutions that Regulus provides.

What is the Problem?
Landfills, Incineration, Garbage dumps:

- Landfills have 5 major problems:
    - Leachate – pollutes the land, ground water, and waterways
    - Greenhouse gases – methane (25x worse than CO2)
    - Toxins: mercury, arsenic, cadmium, PVC, solvents, acids and lead
    - MSW breaks down at a very slow rate and remains a problem for future generations
    - Life cycle cost is high
- Incineration is a major polluter: toxins created (dioxins, etc.), smell, significant objections by local residents
- Garbage heaps and uncollected garbage create health hazards – 3rd World

What is the Problem?
Crude Oil Based Transportation Fuels:

- Pollution: SOx, Particulate / Soot, Unburned Hydrocarbons, NOx, CO
- Carcinogenic elements – benzene – from the crude oil – present in the pollution
- Most countries must import energy / transportation fuels; lack of access to energy limits economic, social, and spiritual growth, and is the #1 cause of war

Every Person on the Planet is Affected by these Problems.

Regulus provides a **Redemptive Business Solution** to these pressing problems.

Regulus Plant Designs Provide:
- Reduction in amount of MSW to landfill by 80% or more
  - Leachate, GHG emission, toxin, longevity reduction
- Fuel plant has no exhaust stack – negligible emissions
- Produce cleanest burning jet, diesel, alcohol fuels in world – reductions in emissions by as much as 95% compared to crude oil derived fuels
- No carcinogens (benzene) in the fuels
- Build economies with good paying jobs
- Help nations move towards energy independence

<u>Abundance Economy Model</u>
The Redemptive Business model being used by Regulus in centered on the Biblical worldview that our God desires to bring choice based economic freedom to the nations through the business sphere of influence in order to enable people to build His Kingdom on earth. Included in this is the requirement of good stewardship of the planet first mentioned in Genesis. By applying God-inspired technologies that convert waste streams and renewable feedstocks into energy, both clean burning fuels and electricity, while minimizing or eliminating toxic by-products of current energy production, Regulus will help countries generate their own renewable clean energy sources, provide strong economic benefits to the nation including eventual local majority ownership, and partner with the local communities through benevolent giving programs.

Kingdom Green Energy, LLC (KGE)
Founded by Richard Wurzbacher - 2019

www.KingdomGreenEnergy.com

What is the problem related to waste tires?
In the U.S.A. alone, over 300M end of life tires are removed from service annually. Historically, scrap tires have been discarded in various legal and illegal manners.

Who is affected by this problem?
Any country, state or city having an abundance of waste tires.

What is the current negative Impact?
(In the U.S.A and abroad)

- Increased degradation of land and landfills due to waste tire toxicity.
- Increased degradation of clean air and water, affecting health.
- Increased spread of deadly mosquito disease transmission.
- Increased toxic emissions (sulfur, dioxins and **CO_2** emissions).

What is the solution?
KGE will Implement our scalable/modular waste tire-to-energy pyrolytic conversion technology utilizing multiple processing lines. KGE contributes to four critical areas:

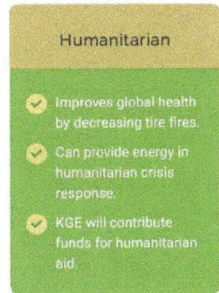

Is the Technology Proprietary or Patented?
The KGE Technology is fully proprietary.

Who benefits?
Any country, state or city possessing an abundance of waste tires.

How:
Communities benefit with new job creation, increased income and a cleaner and safer environment.

Commodity Sales:
Fuel will be sold to refineries. Recovered Carbon will be sold into multiple markets. Buyers for both have been identified.

What does one commercial scale processing line look like as the solution?

The KGE waste tire conversion solution has 4 general steps:

Key Performance Attributes

• Technology lines are modular and scalable for any amount of feedstock processing desired, from a trailer sized unit to full commercial scale facilities.

• Pilot and prototype systems have proven system performance and quality of end result commodities.

• Plant converts waste tires into hydrocarbon crude oil, carbon black and methane.

• Regular maintenance can be performed on individual processing lines independently, thus allowing a true continuous 24/7 full time operation.

• Up to 6M tires can be converted in a full scale plant (60,000 tons annually)

• A plant can produce any amount of fuel, recovered carbon black and methane based on quantity of feedstock processed.

- Unused synthetic gas is recycled back to self-heat and power the reactors.
- Unique state-of-the-art process steps overcome prior art tire pyrolysis limitations.
- Fuel is high quality real hydrocarbon fuel (not bio-diesel).
- Crude oil produced is virtually identical to crude sourced from world ground crude.

Benefits

- Stimulates local economies and business growth wherever plants are placed.
- Creates as many as 65 new full time good paying jobs per facility based on size.
- Financial model is profitable without subsidy and is profitable on day one of production after commissioning of each facility.
- Contributes to providing significant global solutions for real world waste tire environmental hazards.
- Significantly reduces sulfur, dioxins and **CO_2** emissions from hazardous waste tires.
- Stewardship will be a pay-it-forward model, benefiting other Kingdom projects.
- Benevolence will go to local community through foundation or charitable trust.

Extensive Risk Mitigation

- Received excellent technology review conducted by the DOD, U.S. Army Engineering Corp.
- Completed project feasibility study with technology and financial stress tests conducted by a globally recognized professional engineering firm.
- Completed extensive analytical laboratory tests conducted on liquid fuels and recovered carbon black.
- Completed an extensive emissions study on syngas, conducted by globally recognized emissions consultants, resulting in compliance with federal, state and local regulatory statutes.
- Secured feedstock from primary and secondary (backup) feedstock provider.

Abundance Economy Model

The strength of KGE's Abundance Economic Model is through the conversion of waste streams such as hazardous waste tires by converting them into useful products. This completes the cycle of responsible reuse of the original raw feedstock. The financial model is profitable without subsidy, with a strong EBITDA. Each plant creates good paying jobs and offers resources back into the community.

Delta Force Motor
Founded by Michael Kramer 2016

At Delta Force Motors, our vision is to use technology to solve some of the huge problems that face humanity and the planet earth.

With the population of the planet ever expanding, billions of people suffer every minute of every day due to unequal access to energy. Access to energy should be considered a basic human right, as it is required for farming, refrigeration, clean water & sewage treatment, the basic necessities of life!

The current greed driven monopoly of carbon fuels has made it unlikely that alternative fuel sources can make a substantive impact due to a lack of commitment of funding sources to invest the required capital to change the tides in the direction of low cost, clean and abundant energy for all humanity.

We are talking about a planetary paradigm shift and transformation!

How do we get there from here?

We will establish an independently funded private research facility where we are able to conduct the required research and development on advanced, outside the box technologies in clean energy production and other technologies, that we can bring to market in short time frames to better the human condition.

We will employ a dedicated staff of engineering professionals to carry out our R&D activities. The facility will be equipped with the latest cutting edge tools and machinery to facilitate our R&D efforts. Initially, we will be focused on developing next generation technologies in the areas of:

- Extracting useful energy from magnets,
- Hydrogen on demand generation,
- Efficient water desalination and
- Artificial intelligence

<u>Abundance Economy Model:</u> We will actively invest in, and incubate promising technologies by hosting inventors at the lab through our "Inventor in residence program". In order to qualify for this program, an invention must be able to transform the lives of 1bn people.

Neuroscience Centre of Excellence in Accra
Prepared by Ross Dickinson for Korle-Bu Neuroscience Foundation 2020

Introduction: The Project Need and Organization

The Korle-Bu Neuroscience Foundation (KBNF) was established to address the need for improved neurological care in Ghana and the West African region in general.

Founded in 2002, KBNF (www.kbnf.org), has contributed to the overall improvement of hospital care in Ghana and West Africa. Activities range from conducting medical missions, obtaining and shipping surplus hospital equipment and even complete architectural designs for the first large modern teaching hospital in the country (now built!).

The initiative described here is a result of years of effort in the West African Region by KBNF to meet the extensive deficiencies in neurological health services. This initiative seeks to establish sustainable neurological care by fusing prefabricated building techniques, renewable energy and modern high-speed communications together into a small footprint decentralized hospital development that may be replicated throughout the region and beyond.

In addition, great thought has been given to staff training, retention and reward in order to ensure excellence in health care deliver to all. KBNF refers to these facilities as "Hospitals of Excellence". They are expected to have equal or greater impact than KBNF's teaching hospital now functioning in Accra. The goal of sustainable, regional, World Class Health Care and Training in developing countries is within reach.

The urgent need for a new Neuroscience Centre of Excellence in Ghana is well documented herein and elsewhere. Consider this singular fact: In Ghana there is one Neurosurgeon for every 1,250,000 people versus the North American average of 1 to 125,000 people. Opportunity exists to address this extreme disparity in an economically sustainable way.

KBNF has developed a unique model for a small urban or regional hospital (80 to 150 bed) energized by solar, wind and biomass: Hospitals of Excellence are projected to be sustainable (self-powered and self-financed) and earn a return on investment in order to support additional hospitals or allow self-financed expansion. The design includes either fiber optic connections or a large satellite receiver dish to allow continuous high speed video, audio and data linkage to public and private networks. KBNF surgeons and senior health care providers, together with a wide network of other neurological professionals associated with KBNF (including the G4 Alliance) are available to the hospital staff through video conferencing to assist in rounds and surgical procedures 24/7.

This proposal is for an 80 bed neurological care hospital with expansion potential. The hospital is to be located between the Airport and Monrovia. The hospital will be a net generator of power to the local grid, selling excess power to the Government. Income from the power will service the debt and operating costs of the hospital. The hospital will be structured as a franchised co-operative of KBNF. It will have a mandate to meet all standards as set by The Ministry of Health and KBNF, train new medical staff as required to birth additional hospitals in region, and be a guarantor to new independent franchises.

The acute deficiency in neurological health care in Ghana, and indeed all of West Africa, was originally articulated by Dr. Felix Durity, Professor Emeritus at the University of British Columbia and former Head of the Division of Neurosurgery at Vancouver General Hospital. Dr. Durity initially visited West Africa in November 2002 and prepared a *Needs Assessment Report* based on his findings. His report indicated that there was a great deficiency in the current manpower, financial resources, hospital facilities and equipment in the neuroscience area and as a result, patients requiring neurosurgery are either dying prematurely or unable to enjoy life to their full capacity. The situation has improved somewhat over the 12 years since making this assessment, however acute shortages in facilities and trained medical care givers remains. Simple neurosurgical procedures that are routinely performed in Canada are unavailable to the average person of West Africa due to the scarcity of neuroscience resources and high cost.

KBNF, beginning in 2002 to present, is executing a plan to improve the quality of neuroscience care by facilitating a training program to upgrade the skills of Ghanaian, Liberian and other West African neurosurgeons, nurses, paramedicals, pathologists, radiologists, anesthesiologists and neurologists. This additional training in conjunction with regular shipments of high quality equipment and supplies to Ghana and West Africa has begun, along with other initiatives carried out by others, to create a base of competent professionals in support of the new Neuroscience Centre of Excellence facility.

KBNF has fostered enduring relationships with local champions of health care development. For example, KBNF will collaborate closely with Professors Adukhei and Afua Hesse; Dr. Alferd Lutterodt (Queen Elizabeth II Diamond Jubilee Medal recipient) and Dr. Gladstone Kessie founder of Mount Olives Hospital in Ghana to ensure the final designs are appropriate and the core team is in place to operate the hospital once construction is complete.

The first KBNF Neuroscience Centre of Excellence will likely be built in Liberia, within the greater regional district of Monrovia. KBNF has identified a number of sites, but one in particular is being pursued by Dr. Ben Kolie.

The new 80 bed facility will have 3 operating rooms, an imaging unit with x-ray and angiographic suite, an MRI suite and a CT scanner suite. In addition there will be in-house pharmacy, laboratory, rehabilitation and support services. In order to support the retention of staff, a nurses and paramedical residence will be provided in the building for the exclusive use of the professionals at the Neuroscience Centre of Excellence.

An International Residence for visiting consultants is included in the Fourth Floor Layout. These rooms will accommodate visiting experts, recognized in Neurology, Neurosurgery and related Neuroscience fields, who volunteer and/or are sponsored to mentor and teach local personnel. The shared residence will facilitate collegial interaction and foster enduring mutually beneficial and productive relationships. Conference rooms will all be equipped with video conferencing in order to allow follow up seminars and training by KBNF's network of experts with the staff at the Neuroscience Centre of Excellence.

The new Neuroscience Centre of Excellence will be equipped with wireless service throughout. This will allow for fully interactive real-time diagnosis, surgical and post-operative follow up with surgeons living in other countries. Specialized equipment to allow this type of interaction using iPad and Surface equipment is being provided at cost through Tryten. Nursing activities, that require a great deal of mobility, will also benefit from interactive support using equipment as described above and products such a "Go-Pro" that may be integrated into nursing garments. Such interactive gear will allow internationally based senior head nurses to be with their Ghanaian counterpart as their rounds are made, greatly assisting in the ongoing training and general quality of care being given.

The new Neuroscience Centre of Excellence will be equipped with high quality equipment. Maintenance will be done by Liberian technicians trained internationally and assisted via KBNF's network of standby biomedical technicians who will come to the Centre to hold training workshops. Equipment maintenance will also benefit from the high-speed wireless service by providing real-time equipment diagnostics support by remotely stationed biomedical technicians in order to ensure all equipment stays operational.

KBNF is a board member of the G4 Alliance. (www.theg4alliance.org)

As such the leading edge design applied to the Neuroscience Centre of Excellence seeks to meet the many progressive goals established by the G4 Alliance. In addition, in the past, when last being a proponent of this size of hospital development in 2006, KBNF received the support of the Ghanaian Government, the University of Ghana Medical School, the Federation of International Education in Neurosurgery (FIENS), members of the Canadian Congress of Neuroscience (CCNS), the president of the World Federation of Neurosurgery (WFNS), and the International Surgery branch of the Department of Surgery at the University of British Columbia. The list of supporters for this initiative is expected to be similar if not more extensive.

The Favor Path
Invariably, in my experience, Favor follows the act of taking risk of the type originally modeled by Abram (Genius 12). Favor followed risk of two men with a net worth of $10,000 cash to venture off to Ghana in hopes of bringing a solution to the vexing problem of dumping waste openly and seeing it burn freely. The desire was inspired by earlier risk taking in life. For my partner Dave it came from adopting a Ghanaian orphan. For me, it came from having seen first-hand life of the orphan born and dying on a garbage dump in Tanzania years earlier. Favor ensued when sometime later after our return I was forced by Heaven, by powers beyond my realm of control, to meet Marj Ratel, founder of KBNF. A short time later, in 2006 I was asked to become a board member and have remained in that capacity ever since. The Favor on Marj flows throughout KBNF. The way that she is used and the breadth and depth of Favor network are extensive. That is the nature of Favor: for it births from risk and is transferable as further or parallel risk is taken toward common goals. The time and event continuum will fill with Favor as risk upon risk or rather, acts of faith upon faith, are boldly taken as The Spirit leads. We work for the Master of Multiplication after all!

Covenant Relationships and Alignment of Assignments
Covenant Relationships with the core people at KBNF are linked through the Alignment of Assignment. It is the principal of "working together for good". The alignments are watered and provided nutrient as we gather in meetings and execute plans that draw from each other's talents. In other areas I am being introduce to Augmented Reality and Virtual Reality experts that share a passion for bringing these technologies forward in such ways that surgeons and medical experts from around the globe are able to converge as if in the same operating theater to save the lives and livelihoods of many a victim of accidental paralysis or neurological disease.

Agreement and Collaboration
These conditions are natural outcomes where passion and desire to serve are fused with a willingness to commingle talents in the absence of pride or reward.

Abundance Economy Model
In this case, the design at all levels is intended to promote an Abundance Economy Model.

Cooperative Model:

A) This type of structure is well known in the USA and Canada. Every employee in this model is an owner, therefore at the outset, the model empowers each worker with a voice in the cooperative. The constitution of the cooperative demands that the cooperative must Pay-it- Forward by taking risk and underwriting new hospitals by pledging their assets in support of new hospitals, pledging their volunteer time to train members of sponsored Hospitals at their hospital.

B) Members as Family: In this model family is recognized as crucial to Abundance. The model invests in specialized areas that allow each shift to stay at the Hospital and provides a credit system to care for their children, either at the specialized area, or at home. Shift work where on-site accommodations are provided result in Abundance, as often nurses will have to travel 3 to 4 hours a day to get to their 12 hour work shift! In this Model, key members such as nurses need places to rest and restore each night on shift and may need family care while on shift. It means that the Hospital Members need to provide care for dependent children of Nursing Members on a case by case basis: not a one size fits all situation. Management must flex to the Members, not the Members to Management.

C) Pay-it-Inward: Abundance results as all members are rewarded equally as the goals of the Cooperative are met through a profit share and retirement fund.

D) Pay-it-Forward: As new Hospitals are established and profitable, they pay forward by contributing to the new cooperative by sharing risk through the pledging of assets and staff resources for training AND Pay-it-Backwards as recognition that the initial conception, finance and efforts made by Marj and KBNF for their hospital were made without thought of rewards but made in faith, in total attitude of risk, with the knowledge that the Maker who is the Master of Multiplication is just doing what is natural as we operate in an Abundance attitude.

E) Abundance comes when a young father is surgically healed after being knocked off his delivery bike and breaks his back. Instead of becoming a beggar and his family becoming impoverished: life begins again as Daniel is saved from paralysis, without charge, but with a pledge to help the Hospital "Pay back" for the gift of healing he received.

F) Abundance comes from setting up a cooperative that serves the community by ridding it of unwanted materials and of infectious and dangerous materials that are left over due to a broken economic system that surrounds the cooperative. The Hospital solves the local waste problem in a "profitable way" by virtue of a technical design Paid Forward to it by KBNF. The profit is significant. The beneficiary is the Cooperative and each individual that is an employee Member. This allows abundance: because this allows each patient without means to be served at no cost other than a moral commitment to "love back" by "giving back in time or good word or prayer".

G) Abundance comes by serving the ultra-rich and the entitled. In top of the line care and accommodation with room enough for wives, caregivers, security and even children in ultra-comfortable private suites: the wealthy of the nation and region are exposed to love and care that is beyond their expectation with quality of care and surgery that is World Class. They pay very well for what they get, in so doing, Pay Forward since the profits pay for those without means. But Abundance does not stop there: for while guests, it is a time to share stories of risk that tell of why the cooperative that has cared for them exists: because of Pay it Forward risk taken by KBNF. The message? Invite them to Pay Forward more from their abundance, more than the fee they paid to get help in their time of need.

H) Abundance in this model comes from the opportunities that will result from Membership collaboration. As Bio-mechanical engineers innovate and share freely with other cooperatives and then are celebrated and rewarded by Pay it Back and Pay if Forward mechanisms built into the cooperative network. This same principal applies to Nurses and Nero-surgeons.

The Goza Landfill Re-Development, Abuja, Nigeria
Founded by Ross Dickinson 2019

The Goza Landfill is now well within the Abuja Metro Regional District. 100 trucks a day pile up 1,000 tons of mixed waste each day at this dumping ground of 500 acres. Raw black effluent stinking of ammonia, laced with VOC's, arsenic, heavy metals in solution, etc. pour daily into a major river on its way to the Pacific Ocean. Children will be born and die there after scavenging through the discards of this thriving Capital city to a Nation of over 250 Million people unless a change in the continuum is called forth from Heaven.

I am visualizing that the Goza Landfill site will be transformed from the current state to a thriving economically vibrant hub of cooperative development. It is in fact a mine, full of resources on land that properly curated has enormous potential to give life and opportunity to many.

EF WASTE is the nation's leading waste management company. The owner of EF WASTE, Gideon Egbuchulam and I first started our journey together in 1998. A FAVOR connection, Gideon as our agent to various countries from his base in California has expanded. He tells me now; he was so motivated and inspired by our vision to restore landfills that he used it as his impetus to return to his country of origin to transform waste management practices there. We are collaborating now to restore the Goza landfill site with the approval of the Federal Government. The goal is to take ownership of the land at Goza and restore it while recovering resources from incoming waste.

Each African nation I've travelled to included a trip to their landfill(s). So far I have been taken to Tanzania, Zambia, South Africa, Ghana, Mauritania and Egypt and done studies for Kenya, Uganda, Republic de Congo and Nigeria. Each of these countries has a similar transformational development opportunity that once established will be a centre of influence to promote the principals of GRACE and FAVOR in Community (Hybrid) Corporations and Cooperatives energized by a privately held micro-grid giving each organization distinctive competence in the area of reduced power rates, fresh nutrient dense produce and proteins from closed loop aquaponics where the bulk of the fish food is derived from CO_2 / Nitrogen mixes released from energy production boilers and turbines and sent through sunlight reactors that allow algae blooms at hyper-active rates. Many other technical combinations exist to break cycles of poverty: All which will enjoy low energy cost advantages together with advantages of synergy with each other where one operation's waste is another operations input.

Pay it forward practices will involve the support of education, pro-active and reactive health care, youth and community sport and neighbor built affordable housing using building materials recovered from mining and recycling operations (gasification ash).

The Favor Path
I was introduced to Gideon 1998 through a Favor connection that instilled hope in Gideon for his country. However, in this case, Favor is a result of mutual determination, for had one or the other (Gideon or myself) lost our determination to toil for and towards an "Abundance Opportunity" for the following 23 years, then the continuation of this Favor meeting would have been lost. We are not in the "timing" business: We are in the determination to follow the path set before us business!

Covenant Relationships
Covenant denotes a sense of finality or indefinite continuum. In this case, as in most of our business relationships, goodwill and mutual desire to grow together over time cement "covenant". This, in my view is different from other

"covenant" relationships we may be given where both parties feel "called" to be in a life-time relationship such as friendship or a missional pursuit.

Alignment of Assignments
In this case the confluence of opportunity with specific design brought about other Alignments is extraordinary. This is an example of Alignment Convergence: a power sign of FAVOR.

Agreement and Collaboration
The Alignment and Covenant resulted in the renewal of a long-term Joint Venture Agreement to open up the Country of Nigeria for better resource recovery and management on an exclusive basis.

Abundance Economy Model
Pay-it-Forward and Pay-it-Back: the abundance of resources hauled into the 90 hectare site over 15 years at 700 tonne per day and the land itself once restored make it possible to do both as affordable and practical highly efficient plant and equipment are deployed through the cooperative model with interrelated business and social units each benefiting from the outputs of other units in the cluster of development.

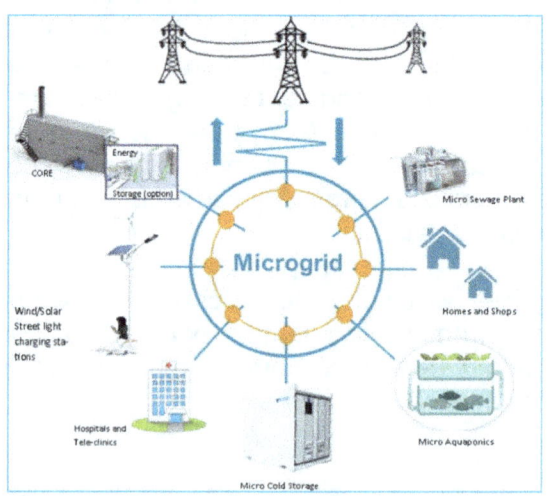

mVillage, A new sharing community where Christians Stay, Pray and Play.
Founded by Sam Piercy, CEO and Joe Piercy 2021

Overview

mVillage was originally the name for the online membership area of my financial education and marketing company called MoneyMinding. This company developed training programs and materials to help people apply entrepreneurial thinking to their financial decision-making. The basis was a 12-step method for building a financial foundation focused on developing purpose-driven cash flow. A key to the program was about developing success in community, and therefore financial professionals and clients from all ages and backgrounds attended programs together so both parties to a financial transaction learned from each other and developed working relationships as a result.

In 2010, this thriving, forward thinking business was raising capital to automate and expand the online community functions. Instead, an unscrupulous "consultant" earned the trust of the board and staff and set about attempting to commit securities fraud with the company. Everything came to a screeching halt from a divine intervention that surely kept me from fighting my way out of jail if the process had completed. The aftermath of this situation has led my husband and I on a journey of continual revelation and deeper trust of God at work in the financial lives of His people.

The new mVillage community is a Kingdom concept for building Christian communities where "Kingdom money, stays and expands the Kingdom" of God in the world today.

Building from the proven "homestay" industry, mVillage connects Christian homes with Christian guests. It also connects Christians who have online and local Christian-friendly activities to share with others online or in their homes or communities. This provides the framework for connecting Christian finances to stay within the Christian community and to be directed towards additional Kingdom projects requiring finances to start or grow.

mVillage hosts receive prayer and practical support including financial and business training. This education provides entrepreneurial and cash flow training so mVillage members will also be able to invest in Kingdom projects and in learning how they can develop a plan to develop their own Kingdom project. The emphasis is on providing interest free financing for real estate, business or ministry activities – all outside of the banking system.

As of the date of this writing, mVillage is beginning its 1st round of equity funding and developing its initial partnerships and covenant relationships.

The Favour / Grace Path

Grace has preserved the purpose and the primary life assets throughout the financial educational/business journey: family, home, health, intellectual property. Favour has opened and closed doors, led me/us to new relationships, as well as ended relationships that didn't align with the direction God was leading us.

One of my favourite discussion topics is discovering mutual connections. I have found that God will go to great lengths to arrange introductions. A couple who my husband and I consider dear friends as well as having a working relationship live 20 minutes from our home in a small town in the interior of British Columbia, Canada. We met this couple through another couple who facilitated a marriage retreat in another part of the country, who were visiting from Texas.

On another occasion, a dear friend and Christian mentor recently chose to end his life through euthanasia. When we received the notice of his decision, we were with a couple we had just met for business purposes. We all lived in different parts of the country, but it turns out the couple we were meeting with knew our friend and his wife more than 30 years earlier before any of them were married. God had orchestrated the timing of the meeting with the new people to provide us with some Christian support during this very sad time.

The list goes on and on: Grace AND Favour through connections to people at just the right time, for just the right purpose.

We were able to produce 2 seasons of a TV show for my MoneyMinding training because we happened to mention the opportunity to someone who connected us to a producer who was interested in finances after he needed to set his video production business aside to take a job in order to be approved by the bank for financing for a new home. He was so awakened to the system, that he was happy to provide his time, equipment and expertise for the opportunity to learn and contribute to helping others learn how to navigate the financial system successfully.

Covenant Relationships

This area of the abundance economy is a tough one for me because, ultimately I would say that the reason the original MoneyMinding business failed wasn't because of the attempted fraud, but because a long-standing covenant relationship ended abruptly. My best friend and business partner (although this relationship was never formally established) had been with me from the beginning. Aside from my husband, she was the person I trusted the most. When I stopped the funding process (a decision which ultimately stopped the illegal activity from completing) my friends' husband gave her an ultimatum: him or me and the business. It later turned out that he was having an affair and their marriage sadly ended, but the influence of her non-involved spouse on the business activities was an important lesson to learn.

For many years I worked alone, and for brief periods of time had people filling roles or wanting to come on board and partner with me. A number of years ago a friend said that these relationships were hard for me because I was operating on a covenant basis and most people operate on a contractual basis in business. That revelation was also life-changing.

Since that time there has been a greater measure, and different degree of prayer and discernment used when entering into new business relationships. I / we have learned that the contractual element of business relationships will flow out of covenant, and that contracts are an important, strategic tool for helping discern any potential red flags before entering into a business relationship.

We have learned that it's not enough to agree on the task, but words and actions need to align as well. Power struggles or personal agendas are best flushed out, not in the words of an agreement, but in the communication and respect given to working through agreement details. A covenant relationship, in my experience is demonstrated by respectful, transparency in communication; if there's a hint at manipulating for some level of control in a relationship, or from an alternate influence over the person we're entering relationship with, we have learned that it's usually better to not proceed. This is one reason we like to connect with husband and wives and wherever possible to connect over a meal at some point early in our discussions. We believe that honesty and transparency in communication are the keys to establishing covenant working relationships, and that even if the work is with one spouse, that it's important to know both spouses because of the marriage covenant each of us has.

Alignment of Assignments
For many years I have shared that it seems easier to talk about sex, than money, unless someone is talking about 'making a killing' somewhere with an investment. In church circles money is such a taboo subject that many churches have chosen not to talk about it. Others adamantly oppose churches who do speak on the subject. When finances are discussed in church circles, they are primarily discussed in connection with God's Word on giving. Great, but what about earning? Some organizations have developed 'Christian' financial training, but what I have learned in over 30 years studying and working in and around finances has confirmed that the overwhelming message about finances to the Christian church is not much different than applying scripture to the financial planning strategies taught through the financial industry. These strategies focus on accumulation as the pinnacle of wealth, and denounce debt, without the corresponding training on credit.

I can go on for hundreds of pages on this subject, the point is that I learned early on, that teaching people how to get rich is actually relatively easy. Non-Christians don't have guilt and shame over, or make justification, for their financial situation the way many Christians do. This has created many challenges since most Christians I've met who love God and love the Kingdom Financial strategies, recognize the need, but aren't prepared to give up a paycheque to pursue an entrepreneurial venture to benefit others.

The other issue has been an undertone of arrogance or pride for many people who wear their Christian 'no debt' status, or their ministers title as a badge of honour. I also see the reverse, which is a denial or fear of what others will think if they start talking about money– even though everyone agrees it's a topic that is much needed. It's quite a conundrum that has been the subject of much prayer!

What is the answer? Who is receptive? How do you reach an audience that wants and needs finances, but is afraid of being judged for wanting to know more, or pursue more finances? Yet, it's obvious you can't keep squeezing money when the field isn't being replanted. The relentless pursuit in prayer and discussion for the alignment for the assignment has led to much growth and learning.

mVillage is the result of continuing to pursue God's constant nudging to keep going. In an instant, rather that people shying away, they are asking to help. Why? Because mVillage 'checks all the boxes' in terms of meeting immediate needs in a way that is non-threatening to someone's belief system, or current situation. mVillage enables people worldwide to connect in a way that breaks through economic barriers and perceived differences that finances have exemplified within the Church. mVillage also enables Christians from various theological backgrounds and doctrinal positions to come together with a common purpose – to connect with other believers and share quality time and finances to benefit the Kingdom of God in their homes, communities, nations and around the world – to love God, love each other, and bless others.

Agreement and Collaboration
The value of a written goal is clearly articulated in scripture and verified in science. Many years ago, I implemented a practice of asking my financial planning clients to write in their own words what we were implementing. This practice brought clarity to our conversations and removed the tendency for a client to nod in agreement with only a partial understanding. This later became part of a process of engaging clients in the financial planning discussions and recommendations. They felt respected and our communication was clear, and by default we laid a foundation for a solid, respectful, profitable relationship.

I later expanded the concept of writing expectations and understandings before meetings and upon agreement for all sorts of business transactions – from simple ones like renewing household insurance, to contracting with marketing firms, for example.

Recently this practice proved valuable in ending a relationship with a firm who insisted they hadn't promised certain targets and activity. The notes were supported by recordings of our meetings and their communication trying to justify their changing position.

Some of the areas that were addressed in the informal 'notes of understanding' were somewhat subjective, seemingly small issues, but later proved to be an indication of a relationship that was not aligned – an unequally yoked, not covenant agreement, despite the initial excitement and common values. Some of these subjective issues were type of communication, frequency of communication, and response time to questions asked. The lesson is that any jostling for a power position in business relationships doesn't contribute to a rising abundance economy.

Abundance Economy Model
The simple basis for the mVillage model is to make sure that everyone who participates receives tangible value. If you are a Christian and you purchase services from a Christian, both of you get value. If you are a Christian and you have money to invest, you expect your funds to contribute to supporting the Kingdom of God on earth. You also expect your funds to be secure, and to receive a return on investment. Rethinking abundance, means rethinking these things as well as to value cash flow (income generation) over growth, so that growth in asset value becomes a by-product of cash flow.

The biblical basis for this is small seeds being used to produce small harvests. Each harvest produces something to eat, something to share, and something to replant which multiplies the investment of time and money easier and faster than funds that are sitting idle and not producing immediate and ongoing income that contributes to the current needs of individuals and businesses. The 'flow' of money, rather than the accumulation of funds in storehouses, is what fuels economic momentum, with less dependency on credit.

The sharing economy built on this mindset will produce regular small profits from each transaction. Funding the Kingdom with the mVillage model means that the profits and any specific designated funds will create a funding pool. Training will help students develop plans that will contribute to this Kingdom economy and will enable them to receive interest free funding for real estate, business, ministry, or any project requiring additional cash to help someone get free from bondage of the conventional banking system, and contribute to the growth of the Kingdom economy.

This abundance model focusing on the flow of funds within the Christian community worldwide is based on a simple method of using existing and well-established systems in real estate and business that don't require complicated strategies or regulatory approval. The mVillage model aims to help reinforce abundance, Kingdom-minded thinking for everyone in the community, at every level as we strive to increase the wealth of others as well as ourselves and live out the direction in Jeremiah 29:7 so that collectively the community prospers and we are better able to help those who need help the most!

AM Ministries
Founded by Brigette Marx 2016

The ultimate goal and purpose of AM Ministries is to play a decisive part in preparing society for the coming Kingdom of God and through fearlessness and devotion we shall not be content with achieving anything less.

We shall also endeavour to expand the Kingdom of God on earth by restoring the relationship between prophets and kings. This monumental task cannot be executed by us as individuals alone; we rely on God's favour and the renewed minds of our fellow believers, to build the Kingdom one willing heart at a time.

THE MARKETPLACE NEEDS TO BE TRANSFORMED; FOR THIS IS THE TIME

*to assemble *to prepare *to advance *harvest *to gather the silver and gold *to build *of victory *to seek deeper spiritual dimensions
*for kings and prophets to corroborate *of wonderworking power *to gain territory
*to gain rulership

"After this manner therefore pray ye: Our Father which art in heaven, Hallowed be thy name. Thy kingdom come. Thy will be done in earth, as it is in heaven." Matthew 6:9-10

AM Ministries presents various courses and training to assist the body of Christ to grow in spiritual authority, understanding and wisdom in strategy to overcome and to grow in maturity. This enables the child of God to be successful in their God given destinies and assignments on earth.

The following is a list of some of the current courses presented:

1. Kings

Assisting kings (Business leaders) with their task in establishing Gods Kingdom Economy on earth through equipping and empowering them spirit soul and body.

Some of the subjects focused on:

a. God's Kingdom Economy (what is happening with the world's economy, what is the Lord doing and what is your function to aid in God's Kingdom success on earth?)
b. Birth right and authority of a king
c. Spiritual Realm opposing the success of your business (Belial, Jezebel, Leviathan, Fear)

d. Your Business or Kingdom as a Spiritual City (Build, Defend and Strengthen)
e. Spiritual Governance – Built your Business or Kingdom compared to Biblical Israel's Government
f. Legislate Spiritual Law to protect your kingdom or business against the corrupt system

2. Queens

Assisting the wife's and daughters of kings to understand their function, role, authority and dominion within all dimensions to aid in the task of building and securing Godly "kingdoms" on earth.

Some of the subjects focused on:

a. The authority and identity of a Queen
b. Function and Role of a Queen within a kingdom
c. Character and nature of a Godly Queen
d. Protecting and raising up your Princes and Princesses according to the ordinances of the Lord

3. The Heavenly Courts

The main objective of the seminar is for the child of God to gain an overview pertaining to the complete and strategic navigation within the Heavenly Courtrooms, whereby the children of Light are properly prepared and equipped to advance the Kingdom of God by applying revelation knowledge, and in doing so with success, defeat the enemy.

This will be achieved by becoming familiar with the following categories regarding the Heavenly Courts:

- the various rules within the Heavenly Courts
- the divine authorities in the Heavenly Courts
- the jurisdictional system
- the authorities of the child of God
- the function and workings of the various Heavenly Courts (Court of Mercy & Grace, Council of Judges, Parliamentary Court, Court of Times & Seasons, International Court, Mountains Court and the Supreme Court) through detailed and practical experiences.

It is also our hope, that this seminar succeeds in delivering the Good News to you, to announce the releasing of the captives, to bring forth recovery of sight to those who are blind, to bring deliverance and victory to the oppressed and to establish Heaven on earth in all your various spheres of influence.

4. The International Guarding Operations Training

This seminar handles on the structure of a city or "kingdom" and how to strengthen it through the application of various prayer strategies. The seminar also defines the different Guarding or prayer positions needed to successfully strengthen and defend your Kingdom or organizations. It is a practical seminar that will assist members to know where they fit into the prayer structure of their kingdom and also how to build such a "spiritual city" or kingdom.

OTHER DIVISIONS WITHIN AM MINISTRIES:

1. SA UNITE IN CHRIST (www.sauniteinchrist.co.za)
CITY ROYALS (In the Process of forming, but this is an entity to assist in the safeguarding, equipping and restoration of the "Royal Families" who are in need of these services and help. Our ministry have been specialized over years to work with business leaders, assisting them in the formulation of spiritual strategies to aid in their success and therefore it has grown to become a whole division within our ministry.

GGA (GLOBAL GUARDING ALLIANCE) This is a Global Apostolic specialized prayer and spiritual force. This movement is formed by members from 29 countries globally and persist of the following divisions:
1. 24 Hour global "Guarding" or specialized prayer team
2. 24 Hour global worship team
3. Apostolic Council
4. Prophetic Council
5. Shepherds Council
6. Research Council (Intel Department)
7. Heavenly Courts Council
8. Agri Council (Specifically focused on protecting farmers and their farms)
9. Decrees Council (writing of decrees in accordance with God's legal and judicial system which then are endorsed by Heavenly Courts Council and enforced through the Global Guarding Team) www.amministries.co.za

The Favor Path
This path began in 2016 when I, Brigette Marx, published my book on Amazon, The Seven Heavenly Courts. John Anderson got hold of the book and contacted me to arrange a skype session. My journey started here with John Anderson. In beginning 2019 I flew to Denver, Colorado to meet with the Marson family and John came to meet me in Colorado. We spent a few days together and during this time John invited me to become part of the GDP family. Through the GDP family I have met Dr. Stan Jeffery and Dr. Gary Sorensen.

AM EDUCATION AND RESORTS (CITY PROJECT)
Founded by Brigette Marx 2018

This project blueprint and idea was encouraged by some friends who prompted me that they believed the Lord wanted me to build a project but I had no idea what the Lord wanted me to build.

I spend time in isolation and worship seeking the Lord for His heart in this regard. The Lord "downloaded" a blueprint into my spirit about a 6-star city to be built in South Africa. This will be both a "city" to become a place of refuge in the future for God's people but also a "showcase" of His goodness to the world.

I worked with a CFO friend to start formulating this business plan and some of the key elements of this City Project are the following:
All spheres of influence are present:

- Educational Hub with courses, schools and programs reaching all ages, communities and all spheres of influence on a spiritual, soul and natural level. (We could possibly become an extended branch of the Abundance Research Institute within this Educational Hub.)

- Media Centre (Publishing, TV and sound studios, marketing etc.)

- Family Park with fun filled and educational events for the whole family this includes a family resort, toddlers, children's and teen's themes parks as well as a water and sports park.

- Business Park which includes conference and boardroom facilities, Innovation and Entrepreneurial Centre etc.

- Arts and Entertainment – Apart from the theme and waterpark we will also be building a 10 000 state of the art theatre to host music and gospel festivals and gatherings.

- 1000 Room 6 Star Hotel with small shops or a "mini" mall hosting 5 different restaurants including a sky roof, sushi bar and lagoon restaurant.

- We will also incorporate special facilities for GDP and their Embassy which will allow and cater for the special security needs and facilities to host GDP events, meetings and to host their political and business guests and partners.

- Wildlife Reserve and Park – This Wildlife resort will have its own chalets, restaurant and other facilities.

- Innovative and Futuristic Farming – Our aim is to assist local farmers and where ever possible expand on local farming with new development to secure food now and for the future.

- Our heart is similar to your module and it is our vision to multiply profits to build up or expand on new and upcoming businesses, fulfill the Law of Christ and our responsibilities towards our communities, employees and those who serve alongside us.

Our intention is to build and secure modules with the help of those like-minded, to secure what we build and erect for 1000 generations to come unto His glory and for His coming rule and reign.

<u>The Favor Path</u>
This path began in 2016 when I, Brigette Marx, published my book on Amazon, The Seven Heavenly Courts. John Anderson got hold of the book and contacted me to arrange a skype session. My journey started here with John Anderson. In beginning 2019 I flew to Denver, Colorado to meet with the Marson family and John came to meet me in Colorado. We spent a few days together and during this time John invited me to become part of the GDP family. Through the GDP family I have met Dr. Stan Jeffery and Dr. Gary Sorensen.

Painting by Gary Sorensen Age 12

Angy Beurskens Stylist & Designer BV
Founded by Angy Beurskens and Andrea Demel 2019
www.angybeurskens-stylist-designer.com

The Company
We are living in a broken world ravaged by wars, violence, terrorism, fear, poverty and a consistent decrease or destruction of moral values. Angy Beurskens Stylist & Designer felt urged to implement words, designs with bible verses that have depth of meaning and bring assurance in the power of God's words. Angy Beurskens Stylist & Designer B.V sees itself with its products as a support concerning a recollection on Jesus Christ and the faith on God in the Bible. Angy Beurskens Stylist & Designer B.V is not a religious Institution.

THE BRAND
SOOTHY is representative of a natural style, the things that make one feel good. Soft, fresh, clean, gentle, cosy but with pieces that have an inner depth and outward power. Pieces, that envelope you in a sense of comfort and love and bring that deep ultimate rest we all long for. For us it is about the inner rest of the soul as well as the outward rest of the mind and body. Our faith in God is integral to who we are and our pieces reflect this. We design bed linen with bible verses that have depth of meaning and bring assurance in the power of God's words.

The Vision
The plan is to establish a new product line into an already existing market. It will embody and distribute a variety of products starting with bed linen but later, bathrobes, nightwear, towels, clothing and gift items. Inspired by the word of God – the Bible – and the power it holds, our designs are of the highest possible quality, thus honouring and exalting God as well as those who will come into contact with the products. Elegance, simplicity, luxury and comfort will apply to all our designs regardless of the age we design for.

Indeed, our designs span across all ages and are gender neutral. Our label Soothy, provides the opportunity to be in visual and physical contact with the word of God.
Our philosophy is: "Evangelism through Textile design"

Bill Gates once had a vision for every household to be supplied with a PC. Today we live in a world where computers are not to be ignored, as they have become an essential part in our lives. We have a vision that every home, hotel, hospital and hospice will have access to the word of God. Whether through a bible or other products, our desire is to facilitate a way that inspires a love for God's word and a relationship with God himself. Our designs epitomise this desire.

The MISSION

Our mission is for the Kingdom of God to be advanced. The mission is to open new doors for the word of God to enter every home, also hotels and hospitals, and with other product lines planned, to even more facilities. The aim is to create spiritual contact points for divine spiritual covering. The mission is creating a way for the presence, the anointing of God to be released into people's homes or other facilities, by contact points such as bedlinen that has been pre -prayed over, blessed and prophesied over by divine selected vessels, Prophets of the Lord, after the products are manufactured.

Matthew 11:28 "Come to me, all you who are weary and burdened, and I will give you rest."

Abundance Economy Model: We are Awake and following the FAVOR path, building Covenant Relationships, looking for the Alignment of Assignments to come into Agreement for Collaborations that will reveal our Abundance Economy Model.

Chapter 9
Conclusion

When most people think of the word Abundance they may think of surplus or increased profitability and prosperity. We do not consider that Abundance provided resources for the creation of the cosmos or the cells in our body or the breaths we take each day.

The Abundance Economy is not about creating opportunities for more profitability and surplus but it is about creating opportunities for God's goals for our freedom. Abundance is an invitation from God to colaborate and co-labor with Him in His vision for His people. God the creator of the Garden of Eden for us, has always intended for us to live and operate in His Abundance Economy, and the invitation still stands.

Abundance has been written about for centuries but the revelation of the timing of a coming Abundance Economy is relatively recent. Jeanne House spoke of the Rising Threshold of Abundance in January 1813 and Dr. Eduard Heimann wrote about the Economy of Abundance in January 1957.

In both my research and my personal search I found Abundance values that are important to understand before entering into the Abundance Economy. Here are a short summary of the Abundance values. From my vantage point my observations and perspectives reveal that the structure of the Abundance Economy is different from past eras. To describe what I am seeing I am using my own new terms such as the Favor Path, Covenant Relationships, Alignment of Assignments, Agreement & Collaboration, Awakening Consciousness, and the Abundance Economy Models.

The Favor Path
Although many people go through life viewing everything as a matter of good or bad luck, the Favor Path connects us to our years of preparation (which can even be generational) to our inspired visions to our interlink with others at the appropriate time. A frequency of Favor acts like a magnet to attract people on the same frequency and accelerates the building of relationships. Favor is not an event but a process that cycles through us.

Covenant Relationships
The Favor Path may have intersections that lead to invitations to build Covenant Relationships. Devoting quality time for fellowship is important for building Covenant Relationships. Lack speaks of delay, postponement and failure. Abundance speaks of preparation using a concert of Covenant Relationships. Covenant Relationships can exponentially increase the impact of Favor and the power of agreement. The Favor Path may introduce

individuals first who are open and willing to enter into the foundations of Covenant Relationships before one seriously explores the potential of Agreement and Collaboration for projects. Discernment is a safety valve in building Covenant Relationships. The Favor Path intersections may act as both a collector and connector of Covenant Relationships. Covenant Relationships are a byproduct of Favor and an invitation that need to be acted upon.

Alignment of Assignments

Finding proper Alignment of Assignments requires you to know why and where to look and who to look for in your search. Short cuts will short circuit the Abundance outcomes. Complimentary visions can be enhanced by the alignment of assignments.

Stewardship of the alignment of assignments not ownership of assignments is a key for seed planting of visions in the Abundance Economy. Natural Alignment of Assignments may make smooth transitions into the values of the Abundance Economy.

Agreement and Collaboration

Agreement with God's vision is more powerful than Agreement with our own vision. The power of Agreement is stronger than the power of control. The torch of Agreement and Collaboration can be carried from the Lack Economy into the Abundance Economy by declarations of blessings. Do not let your power of Agreement and Collaboration be limited by the obvious. Sharing a common vision along with sharing Abundance values and sharing a frequency communication can accelerate coming into Agreement and forming Collaborations.

Awakening Consciousness

The Abundance values of Favor, Covenant Relationships, Alignment of Assignments, Agreements and Collaborations must all be applied within the context and activation by an Awakening Consciousness. Without Awakening, the Abundance Economy will not seem plausible and will remain invisible to most. The Awakening Consciousness reveals that a few Innovators and Early Adopters of the Abundance Economy are beginning to appear.

Abundance Economy Models

Abundance Economy values are applicable to both small and large businesses. As both the public and the business community see the success in financial, social, environmental and humanitarian Abundance, the template will be replicated. The early adopter Abundance Economy Models are the following: *Pay It Forward by Legacy Collaborators, Seed Money for Equity, Profit Sharing Collaborations, Community (Hybrid) Corporations, Redemptive Business, Inventors in Residence Program, Cooperative Model and Flow of Funds Model.*

Abundance Companies and Organizations
Unlike the present Lack Economy that is fueled by debt and loan obligations, the Abundance Economy is fueled by value assets, seed equity, profit sharing, barter contributions and collaboration. Rather than Pay It Back loans it embraces Pay It Forward sustainable investments. We will follow the learning curve and success of the 21 Abundance Companies and Organizations profiled and add new early adopters in future updated versions of the Rise of the Abundance Economy.

Prints of Original Art Available at: Sorensen-Gallery.Pixels.com

ACKNOWLEDGEMENTS
Sue Sorensen
Leif Sorensen
Professor Dan Zaslavsky
Joseph Fournier
Dr. Som Mitra
Michael Kramer
Kurt Grossman
Wolf Hilbertz
Harold Sorensen
Peter Sorensen
Severine Sorensen
Dr. Stan Jeffery
Dr. Karl Bandlien
John Anderson
Drs. Mark and Jill Kauffman
Kevin and Tami Barthen
Carter Dye
Thomas Meade
Glenn Thomas
Sonya Waters
Tim Stewart
Ross Dickinson
Roelie Etsebeth
Dr. Dan Nold
Brigette Marx
Gary Lovelace
Howard Selman
Randy Horsak
Dr. William Hinn
Dr. Ed Turose
Richard Wurzbacher
Sam and Joe Piercy
Angy Beurskens
Andrea Demel

www.ingramcontent.com/pod-product-compliance
Lightning Source LLC
Chambersburg PA
CBHW070642220526
45466CB00001B/254